THE TWELVE
MONOTASKS

THE TWELVE MONOTASKS

DO ONE THING AT A TIME
TO DO **EVERYTHING** BETTER

THATCHER WINE

Little, Brown Spark
New York Boston London

Little, Brown Spark
Hachette Book Group
1290 Avenue of the Americas, New York, NY 10104
littlebrownspark.com

First Edition: December 2021

Little, Brown Spark is an imprint of Little, Brown and Company,
a division of Hachette Book Group, Inc. The Little, Brown Spark
name and logo are trademarks of Hachette Book Group, Inc.

The publisher is not responsible for websites (or their content)
that are not owned by the publisher.

The Hachette Speakers Bureau provides a wide range
of authors for speaking events. To find out more, go to
hachettespeakersbureau.com or call (866) 376-6591.

ISBN 978-0-316-70554-7
Library of Congress Control Number: 2021945122

Printing 1, 2021

LSC-C

Printed in the United States of America

In memory of my grandparents—

Bessie, Morrie, Gracie, Jack, IW, & Lil.

With immense gratitude for

the gift of their attention.

CONTENTS

CONTENTS

THE **TWELVE**
MONOTASKS

PREFACE

I was deep into researching and writing this book in March 2020 when the coronavirus pandemic arrived in the United States. The world was thrown into chaos overnight and life was intense for just about every person on the planet.

Yet with all the craziness, I felt strangely calm. It's not that I wasn't scared. I was worried about my health—I had gone through cancer treatment two years earlier, which put me in a high-risk group if I were to catch the virus. I was concerned about my family's safety and well-being. I was also stressed about Juniper Books, the business I run, and our ability to survive an economic downturn.

I considered furloughing my team and putting the business into hibernation while I concentrated on keeping myself and my family safe and healthy. In recent years, I had worn myself down as I pushed through multiple health challenges, business struggles, and a divorce while keeping up a busy life as an entrepreneur and father. Maybe this crisis was different—I wondered if I should take a break and not try to do it all this time.

I also briefly considered putting this book on hold. My schedule was packed—could I really fit one more big thing on my to-do list?

I thought a lot about it, then I decided to go a different route.

Even though there were a lot of things that were out of control in the world, what I realized was that I was still in control of my attention and I could choose to apply it where I wanted. I decided to double down on my commitment to monotasking everything in my life. I would do one thing at a time, and I'd do it well. In the chaotic stressful times of the pandemic, I would pressure-test the concepts covered in these pages in order to get them ready to share with the world.

Throughout the pandemic, I read printed books to build my focus. I walked three times a day to get fresh air. I worked on my listening skills with my friends and family. I wasn't sleeping well, but I committed to finding ways to get more sleep every night. I didn't have a lot of time for meals, but as I ate, I contemplated how grateful I was for essential workers on the front lines. I couldn't travel, but I paid attention to things I had never noticed on my way to work. I relearned how to play piano at home by watching You-Tube videos. In our daily company calls, I taught my team how to get our work done from home. I made time to play with my kids and with my dog. I created new ideas for my business every day—some worked, some didn't. I spent a lot of time thinking about what lay ahead and how to help keep everyone in my life safe.

My efforts to monotask were successful. If I tried to do more than one thing at a time during the pandemic, my stress level increased rapidly, and I rarely got anything done. In contrast, when I held the line, stayed focused, and monotasked, I was more relaxed and much more productive. My family stayed healthy, and I was able to finish writing this book. Plus, Juniper Books thrived as people read more books and redecorated while staying at home.

Now, more than ever, I believe that the antidote to our ever-expanding to-do lists, the distractions of modern life, and the fragmentation of our attention is to *do one thing at a time*. Once we realize that *we* are the ones who control our own attention, *we* can choose where to apply it. Monotasking is all about reclaiming our attention so that we can better work through our to-do lists, improve our relationships, *and* get through some very difficult times.

PART I

AN INTRODUCTION TO MONOTASKING

INTRODUCTION

n recent years, the lives we live seem to be getting busier and busier. Technology has increasingly made its way into every part of our existence — nearly everyone has powerful smartphones in their hands, pockets, or somewhere close. Economic and societal pressure has increased the need, or at least the perception, that we should always be doing and striving for more.

Like many people, I've tried over the years to counterbalance the busy-ness and stress of adult life with practices such as meditation, mindfulness, and yoga. I love these practices, but quite often, making time to meditate and go to yoga is challenging. When I'm super busy and need to get a lot of stuff done, being reminded to meditate can be annoying — even if meditating will help (which of course it will, but it's hard to recognize that in the moment).

As a result of the tension between a busy schedule, a busy mind, and all the stress-relieving and self-improvement activities I want to do, these practices have at various times made me feel like I'm simply not very good at them — or that I'm not good at making the time they require. I started to wonder if there was another way to live a balanced life that could be practiced *while* we go about our daily activities, not something that was separate from them.

When I looked back at when I have been the most successful

and happiest in life, I saw a common thread. It was when I did one thing at a time and really paid attention to what I was doing and who I was with. It was not when I tried to do it all at once or when I was distracted and only partially present. Even going through difficult times—cancer, divorce, closing a business—when I gave those experiences my full attention, I made it through as well as one could possibly ask for.

To be less stressed, happier, and more productive in life, I determined that I didn't need to go on a retreat, I didn't need to find a guru, and I certainly didn't need to keep adding to my to-do list.

The book you hold in your hands started with the epiphany that if I gave my full attention to one thing at a time, I could do it well and I could enjoy it more. I needed to stop *multi*tasking and start *mono*tasking.

Now, if monotasking were as easy as just telling you to go do one thing at a time instead of multitasking, this would be a short and not very effective book.

The truth is, monotasking muscles need to be trained and strengthened. Our constant state of busy-ness and attempted multitasking have caused these monotasking muscles to atrophy, making it likely we will become distracted by the sound of one more notification or the "need" to respond to one more email. With strong monotasking skills, you can identify potential pitfalls and actively avoid them.

The way we build our monotasking muscles is to do the things that we already do every day, but to approach them with renewed focus and commitment. There are twelve monotasks that form the core of this book—and they in turn form the core of our lives.

The Twelve Monotasks You'll Find in This Book:
1. READING
Reading focuses our eyes and our brains in one place. By putting our phones down and picking up a printed book, we are choosing to

monotask. Anyone who opens *The Twelve Monotasks* is already practicing the first monotask—reading—and therefore on their way to monotasking success!

2. WALKING

Walking reconnects our bodies to our surroundings. While it may seem like a simple activity, many people view walking as a means to an end, not the end in itself. By focusing attention on our surroundings—what we see, what we hear, how the ground feels under our feet—we naturally reconnect with our overall presence in the world.

3. LISTENING

Listening connects us to others, engaging our auditory senses and our brains. Can you feel when someone actively hears you instead of just pretending to listen? We can all tell when someone is not really present, and it hurts. When we truly listen, whether it is listening to our kids, in a meeting, or out on a date, we connect to other people infinitely better than if our minds are distracted by trying to multitask other thoughts and actions.

4. SLEEPING

Sleeping resets our bodies and our brains so that we can be healthy and have the physical and mental energy we need to thrive. Many people have trouble sleeping these days—we all have a lot on our minds, our days are busy, and our to-do lists are long. What if we could monotask sleep? What if we gave ourselves permission to get the rest and recovery we need? Bringing focused attention to sleep can have benefits that permeate our lives.

5. EATING

Eating is an essential daily activity that is often pushed to the background instead of being given our full focus. We sometimes rush through meals because we need to get back to work, or we don't really pay attention to what we are eating because we're also looking at a device. What if we brought our attention to the food on our table, how it got there, who prepared it for us, what it tastes like, and the companionship provided by those sharing this experience with us?

6. GETTING THERE

What if during our commutes and travels, we focused on the act of getting somewhere and enjoying it instead of feeling like we always have to do two things at one time, often at great risk to ourselves and others? While the time spent in transit can present an opportunity to multitask, there are ways we can bring our attention to the journey and reap the benefits of being more present.

7. LEARNING

We are all capable of lifelong learning: it isn't something we do only in our younger years. When we monotask learning, we encounter one of the most invigorating parts of being human—making new cognitive and emotional connections. Whether we are learning a new language, a sport, or something related to our work, the ability to bring our focus to one thing at a time improves our capacity to learn and unlocks our nearly infinite potential.

8. TEACHING

Teaching strengthens our brains and builds a connection to others. It is not a task limited to classrooms; there are opportunities to teach throughout our lives. One of the best ways to master a skill or subject is to teach it. Preparing to teach requires intense focus and recognition of the limitations of our own knowledge. This chapter explores both the practical elements and emotional aspects of mastering a subject and then conveying it to another person.

9. PLAYING

Playing involves letting go of much of the intense concentration required for the previous tasks, relaxing our brains, and fully inhabiting our bodies. Many adults simply don't allow themselves time to play. Often, we feel guilty when we take time for ourselves or we feel like we are wasting time if we are not being productive or "monetizing" our time. This chapter reminds us that it's okay—and ultimately productive—to have fun.

10. SEEING

Seeing integrates our visual senses. In this monotask, we practice looking both at the details close up, and farther and farther into the world. Instead of worrying about capturing Instagrammable photos, what if we see for ourselves the beauty and complexity of the world around us? How much does our understanding of an otherwise common object change when we stop to really inspect it?

11. CREATING

Creating is one of the most magical and empowering monotasks. You do not have to be an artist or musician or have a creative professional title to be a creator; we are all creators in some capacity. Sometimes the things we create are small, like a note to our children, and sometimes they are large, like starting a new company. The act of bringing something into the world that did not exist before is rewarding. By monotasking the act of creating, we can embrace our unique, limitless possibilities.

12. THINKING

Most of us never think about thinking because we are doing it nonstop, using it to fuel our everyday activities. What if we isolated thinking as a separate task all on its own? Could our dedicated thinking time help us achieve excellence? Monotasking thinking also brings attention to where we have outsourced some of our cognitive tasks to devices and other people in recent years, and how we can reclaim the most important thinking tasks.

How to Use This Book

The twelve monotasking chapters outlined above are the heart of this book. Each is packed with guidance about how to do that one task with your full attention. I recommend reading one chapter, then taking the time to practice that monotask before moving on to the next one.

In addition to the ideas and guidance you find within this book, I created a website—**monotasking.tips**—where you can find even more information, insights, and recommendations. You read the website address correctly, it ends in "tips"—as in a small but useful piece of practical advice.

With twelve tasks, you can dedicate a day, a week, or a month to each task—whatever works for you. I have tried to keep the book user-friendly, with short, easily digestible sections, arranged in the same order in each chapter. You may naturally find it easier to perform one task or another with your full focus, but don't give up on monotasking overall if some monotasks are particularly challenging.

The philosophy contained in this book reflects both my personal experience and that of others who have monotasked their way to success and happiness. Most people have not used the term "monotasking," but I'll demonstrate how they, and you, have monotasked many times without even knowing it.

Perhaps the best thing about monotasking is that it can be applied to every aspect of your life *while* you live it. The more you monotask, the better at it you will become—and you will be able to monotask *more* of your life with greater ease.

THE ART AND SCIENCE
OF MONOTASKING

monotask | (ˈmɒnə, tæsk) / *verb*
to perform one task at a time

While "monotasking" may not be a household term yet, the concept is inherently familiar to us for one simple reason—we all know what *multitasking* is.

Multitasking is when you *attempt* to do multiple things at the same time. Monotasking is the opposite—you do one thing at a time.

Throughout this book, I describe *how* to monotask in a variety of ways, but the foundational approach remains the same: Strip everything away until you have one thing left. *Do that one thing with all your focus.*

In order to become good monotaskers, we need to unwind and break apart our multitasking habits—everything from checking our phone notifications while having lunch with a friend, to answering emails while participating in a Zoom call, to thinking about what happened at work today while playing with our kids.

By isolating individual tasks, you'll become aware of what it looks and feels like to pay attention to one thing. Don't be surprised if this feels foreign to you when you first practice it. It's a feeling we may not have experienced much in recent times.

We can elect to combine various tasks later if we choose, but when we do so, we will be equipped with a new awareness of the difference between monotasking and multitasking. The purpose of this book is *not* to make you feel bad about multitasking. We all live in the twenty-first century: We're navigating rapid changes together, and we all face the same challenges.

The Roots of Multitasking

The word "multitasking" was reportedly first used in 1965 to describe how an IBM mainframe computer could perform multiple tasks at the same time. A few decades later, as personal computers entered the mainstream, people started using the word more frequently to describe both how they, and their computers, could work on multiple things simultaneously.

Apple's Macintosh computer was introduced in 1984 and came with 128K of RAM (random-access memory)—that's a tiny amount of processing power in today's terms. PCs back then would generally crash if you tried to get them to do more than one thing at a time. I frequently feel like one of those early computers when I take on too much at once.

With the release of Microsoft Windows 2.0 in 1987, millions of business users got their first visual representation of what multitasking looked like. One could toggle between applications that performed very different functions—a word processor and a spreadsheet, for example. A new era in multitasking computers, a multitasking workplace, and a multitasking culture had begun.

The introduction of personal computers in the 1980s was followed by rapid growth of the internet in the 1990s and near universal adoption of smartphones in the 2000s. With each step in the technology revolution, our expectations increased—not only of our devices, but also of ourselves. If computers and phones were becoming faster and more powerful every year, shouldn't the human brain be able to keep up? And if computers designed by people could multitask, couldn't people learn to multitask just like them?

The Downside of Technology

Here we are, well into the twenty-first century and decades into the technology revolution. The reality is that we are working more and experiencing more emotional and psychological ups and downs as we make our way into the future. We are more connected and more reachable than ever before. No matter where we are on the planet, emails and texts come in at all hours of the day. Even when we take a break, we still work—according to Project: Time Off, 73 percent of employees work while on vacation.

With the rise of social media, so, too, has there been an increase in reports of anxiety, depression, and loneliness. For a large portion of the population, fear of missing out (or FOMO) is a real thing. Users compare their lives to what they are seeing in the social media feeds of others and often feel never-ending pressure to keep up by working more, spending more, and doing more.

We are all constantly trying, or pretending, to process massive amounts of information. A 2011 study in the *Proceedings of the National Academy of Sciences* reported that while we can cope with the inflow of sensory information, it comes at a cost. "We've identified a kind of bottleneck in the prefrontal cortex of the brain that forces people to address problems one after the other, even if they're doing it so fast it feels simultaneous," says René Marois, PhD, associate professor of psychology and neuroscience at Vanderbilt University and coauthor of the study. "This explains why previous data shows brain activity going down instead of up with each new challenge—it's like a mental traffic jam."

Technology has certainly improved our lives in many ways, but it has come at a cost. It can be hard to put a finger on exactly what that cost is, perhaps because of our own mental traffic jam, but we can feel it. We know we can do better and feel better, but where do we begin?

THE ART AND SCIENCE OF MONOTASKING

The Infiltration of the Present Moment

Up until the early 1990s, there was a certain daily rhythm to most people's lives. School took place at school, work was done at work, dinner happened around the dinner table, and leisure time that included television watching, radio listening, and book reading usually took place in the evenings and weekends. There were very few opportunities to do these activities outside of their usual time and place and so we did them one at a time.

As devices have proliferated and smartphones have become attached to us in recent years, we have the ability to do just about anything we want, anywhere we want, anytime we want. Further, we can seemingly combine as many things as we want into the same moment.

While the internet and our devices may be recent introductions to our lives, the difficulty that humans have staying in the present moment is nothing new. Philosophical and religious traditions have long guided us back to the present moment via prayer and meditation, and for good reason. The present moment is where everything happens and it is the only place where we are truly connected to ourselves, others, and the universe.

Nevertheless, it is our human tendency to always be thinking about the past and the future—we try to make sense of what has already happened, and we ponder what is to come. Then we add incredibly powerful devices to our lives, flood our senses and brains with massive amounts of information, and our present moments become truly jam-packed.

It has become substantially *harder to stay* in the present moment. And, it has become substantially *easier to try* to do more than one thing in that present moment.

The Attention Economy

Where does our attention go during a typical day? How many times do we pick up our phones? How often do we check our texts and emails? How frequently do we log on to social media, use apps, play games, watch the news, or just browse the internet?

All those glances at our phones may be entertaining and informative for us, but they are even more valuable to someone else in the "attention economy." Our attention is a prized possession, and yet we tend to give it away for free, perhaps on the dubious promise of quick entertainment, social connection, information, or something we think we want or need.

In the 2020 Netflix documentary *The Social Dilemma*, Tristan Harris, former Google design ethicist and cofounder of the Center for Humane Technology, repeats a saying that describes how many Silicon Valley giants have built their empires: "If you're not paying for the product, then you are the product." The more attention we give to our devices, the more valuable the companies who are behind the screens become, and quite often, the less we get done.

Our devices don't have feelings (yet!)—if they did, they would be equivalent to the needy narcissistic partner for whom no amount of attention is ever enough. They superficially appear to care about you, give you just enough positive feedback to keep you interested in them, but never genuinely ask how *you* feel about your relationship. You doubt that you should get more serious, but it's too easy to stay.

Monotasking is not about giving up our devices. It's about making the choice for ourselves where our attention goes in every moment.

Let's jump into the twelve monotasks and start building our monotasking muscles.

PART II

THE TWELVE MONOTASKS

TASK 1: READING

I n the spring of 2019, I was exhausted, depleted, and very distracted. For the previous three years, I had been constantly battling and recovering from one thing or another. First it was a hole in my head (true story—more on that later!), then cancer (Non-Hodgkin lymphoma), and then divorce.

All these personal challenges had taken some or all of my attention for a long time. I made it through each one and emerged on the other side, but I was drained—physically, emotionally, and financially. A full recovery would require far more energy, focus, and creative problem-solving than I had ever imagined possible.

While I had kept my business going through all the turmoil, it was now suffering. I started Juniper Books in 2001 and had achieved a long run of growth and profitability. Then came 2017, cancer, hundreds of hours of chemotherapy treatments, and lots of time away from the office. While I was fighting for my life, Juniper Books racked up a substantial loss and experienced a heavy load of office drama that would need time to settle and heal.

After I finished chemo, I wanted to pretend I was fine and that I had my old energy back. However, I was faking it—the truth was, I was beyond exhausted. I wanted to inspire others with my optimism and work ethic, but this time I didn't have the reserves to back it up.

I put in long hours at the office, got up early, and worked late into the night. I was constantly on my phone, on email, and traveling. I was also multitasking nonstop. I was doing all this because I was afraid that the business I had worked so hard to build over eighteen years and keep alive during cancer and divorce would collapse during my recovery.

At the same time, my kids, then ten and twelve, really needed my attention in our new reality of two homes and two parents they saw half the time. They were stressed, anxious, and having trouble sleeping. Night after night, my ten-year-old daughter had panic attacks before bedtime. She didn't want to go to school or on the upcoming spring trip. The arguments and anxiety would escalate every night as bedtime neared.

We tried new approaches to wind down and ease the stress, but nothing seemed to help. We watched shows together, we talked about the day, we made tea, we snuggled with stuffed animals, and I tried to explain rationally how there was nothing to be afraid of. Nothing worked. She was stressed, and I was distracted and thinking about my own problems. That didn't help.

Finally, one night when the arguments at bedtime had escalated again, it seemed like we were heading toward another late and stressful night. She had some reading homework she didn't want to do, so I proposed reading her book to her at bedtime, something I had not done since she was much younger. I picked up her copy of *My Side of the Mountain* and started reading aloud.

No sooner had I started reading the book to her than something magical happened for both of us. Her anxiety subsided and she listened. I focused my mind on reading and didn't think about my work.

That evening in the spring of 2019, we read for twenty minutes. My daughter fell asleep and slept through the night. Every bedtime after that when she was at my home, we read together until we finished *My Side of the Mountain*.

People talk a lot about the intellectual benefits of reading—how you can learn new things and experience the world from the perspective of great storytellers. While we did learn about fourteen-year-old Sam Gribley and how he survived on his own after running away from home, more important, we relearned how to bring our attention to a single point of focus. Our minds were scattered all over the place prior to reading. Once we started the book, they were concentrated in one place.

For my daughter and me, the act of reading calmed our nervous systems. Before picking up that book, the distractions of the world were commanding our multitasking brains to think about this and worry about that. When we returned to life the day after reading each night, we found ourselves much better equipped to tackle one thing at a time. I methodically worked my way through the challenges in my business over the next few months with a newfound focus. My daughter worried less at bedtime and had the experience of a lifetime on the big class trip she had been anxious about.

Reading is one way—one highly effective way—to build mono-tasking muscles. When the distractions of life accumulate, reading is where I always start to bring my focus back and, along with it, my ability to get things done and to be happy.

The Facts About Reading

Humans invented reading a few thousand years ago, points out Maryanne Wolf, a cognitive neuroscientist and child development expert, in her book *Proust and the Squid: The Story and Science of the Reading Brain*. "And with this invention," she writes, "we rearranged the very organization of our brain, which in turn expanded the ways we were able to think, which altered the intellectual evolution of our species."

Books and reading have played a central role in how we have arrived where we are today.

These days, competition for our attention is fierce, and one result is that fewer Americans are reading at all. The Pew Research Center found that 27 percent of Americans had not read a book, in whole or in part, in the previous year. Further, younger people tend to read for less time than older individuals, according to a Bureau of Labor Statistics report from June 2020.

But reading offers tremendous benefits to those who engage in the activity for even a few minutes a day. Ceridwen Dovey, a social anthropologist, wrote in *The New Yorker*, "Reading has been shown to put our brains into a pleasurable trance-like state, similar to meditation, and it brings the same health benefits of deep relaxation and inner calm. Regular readers sleep better, have lower stress levels, higher self-esteem, and lower rates of depression than non-readers."

Reading is also a particularly effective counterbalance to many of the negative effects of other forms of entertainment we consume. Watching television can be overstimulating both visually and auditorily. Keeping up with social media can be stressful. Holding a book in your hands and slowing down to read offers an antidote to digital overload.

One of the reasons that reading may be so good for us is that it guides us back to the present moment where we have to pay attention to one thing in one place. While the content of books often inspires our minds to imagine the past and future via the story on the pages, the act of reading takes place in the *now*. We are nowhere else but reading a book, concentrating all of our attention in the activity and perhaps finding happiness in the present moment where nothing else matters.

Each of the monotasks in this book is about bringing your attention to one thing at a time, then carrying that ability to focus to other activities and throughout your life. When we are tempted to multitask and spread our attention too thin, reading is one of the simplest and most immediate remedies. The attention we give the words on a page will always act as a lighthouse, bringing our mind back in focus.

Dedicated Readers

Some of the world's busiest, most successful people are readers. Not just readers, but prolific readers. How do people like Oprah Winfrey, Reese Witherspoon, and Bill Gates find the time to read dozens of books a year while they run their businesses and foundations, travel, speak, parent, and do all the other things they do? More important, why do they bother reading when they have so much on their to-do list?

Bill Gates is known for starting Microsoft and his dedicated philanthropic work. He also has a bottomless appetite for reading. When he goes on vacation, he brings a tote bag of good old-fashioned printed books and, as of this writing, has not adopted e-reading despite his technological prowess. Reading isn't a hobby Bill Gates has taken on in retirement; it has always been an integral part of his life. In a 2016 interview, Gates said: "Reading is still the main way that I both learn new things and test my understanding."

GatesNotes, Bill's blog, is full of book recommendations and commentary on books he has read. The blog provides a fascinating window into Gates's thinking as well as a great list of books we can put on our reading lists. Gates is obviously a very advanced and fast reader. We may never get to his level of business success or philanthropic impact, but we, too, can read as much as possible as a means to understand the world and develop our ability to have an impact through focused work. These skills can be our pathway for each of us to be more effective in our lives.

For businesspeople, world leaders, and celebrities alike, books offer a source of knowledge and inspiration as well as a refuge to calm the mind and build attention. It's never too late for any of us to adopt reading habits in our adult lives that help us achieve our goals.

|||||||||||||||||||||||||||||||||||||||||||||||||||||||||||||||||||||||||||||||||||||||||||||||||||||||

Nicholas Carr on Physical Books

Nicholas Carr, author of *The Shallows: What the Internet Is Doing to Our Brains*, is one of the best thinkers and writers on the subject of technology and the transformation of modern life. A few years ago, I had the opportunity to talk with him about the past, present, and future of the printed book. He subsequently wrote the introduction for one of Juniper Books' annual printed catalogs, from which I have excerpted the following:

> Why has the physical book endured while so many other media products have been supplanted by digital versions? It's much more than just a matter of nostalgia.
>
> To the human mind, a sequence of pages bound together into a physical object is very different from a flat screen that displays only a single "page" of information at a time. The physical presence of the printed pages, and the ability to flip back and forth through them, turns out to be crucial to the mind's ability to navigate and interpret written works, particularly lengthy and complicated ones.
>
> Even though we don't realize it consciously, we quickly develop a mental map of the contents of a printed text, as if its argument or story were a journey unfolding through space. If you've ever picked up a book you read long ago and discovered that your hands were able to locate a remembered passage quickly, you've experienced this phenomenon. When we hold a physical publication in our hands, we also hold its contents in our

mind. The spatial memories seem to translate into more immersive reading and stronger comprehension.

We live today in an age of distraction, in a constant whirlwind of information and data. The pages of a printed book provide a refuge, a calm place where our minds, freed from the stress of technological overload, are encouraged to connect with deeper thoughts and feelings. Far from being obsolete, the physical book, printed and bound, seems more vital than ever. It is a balm for the harried mind.

Why Monotasking Reading Will Help You Do Everything Better

Reading on a regular basis can be difficult, but it also offers tremendous benefits. Bringing your focus right here to the words on this page—and keeping it here long enough to truly absorb the content—takes some commitment. When you choose to read a printed book, generally the *only* thing you can do is read that book. You can't do anything else while you read, because if you take your eyes off the page you will no longer be reading. If you start thinking about something else, you won't absorb the information from the book.

We should appreciate reading *because* it takes our full focus. Few activities in our contemporary lives require as much concentration as reading. Every time we read, we are building our monotasking muscles for future use in other areas.

For example, reading a science fiction book definitely takes more time and concentration than watching the movie version of the same title. The book might take fifteen hours to complete while watching the movie takes only two hours and little effort. Our attention may wander in both venues, but when we're watching the movie and only sort of paying attention, we can usually absorb enough that the story makes sense and we are entertained. However, with books, if your attention wanders, you may have to go back and begin again where your mind drifted. This is a feature, not a flaw! Reading from the printed page is the first step toward reclaiming our attention, focus, and time.

Other benefits of reading include increasing empathy, decreasing stress, and slowing mental decline as we age. In a 2009 study, researchers at Seton Hall University found that sustained reading (in this case "non-provocative" articles from a magazine) led to lowered blood pressure and heart rate, along with decreased feelings of psychological distress.

According to a study in *Innovation in Aging*, book readers outlived non–book readers by two years. People who read for three and a half hours a week were nearly 25 percent more likely to live longer than those who didn't read at all. Additional research suggests that as we grow older, keeping our brain engaged with activities such as reading helps us maintain and improve our cognitive functions.

 YOUR READING MONOTASK

Read Daily For Twenty Minutes, On Paper

If you've taken a break from reading on a regular basis in recent years, you may find it difficult at first to locate your reentry point. But the great thing about reading is that the more consistently you read, the more you will likely enjoy it and find that giving a book your solitary focus comes naturally.

I consider myself a dedicated reader, but there have been times in my adult life I've gone weeks or months without reading a book. The longer I go without reading, the harder it is to get back into it. Usually, these literary droughts occur when life has become super busy and I've let myself become too occupied with other things.

My reentry point to reading usually begins with short magazine articles (such as Talk of the Town pieces in *The New Yorker*), then longer stories (a *Vanity Fair* article, or perhaps a Hemingway short story), and finally on to an engaging novel or biography. Sometimes I'll read a page turner, such as an easy reading thriller or mystery novel, or I'll reread a book I love. Some of my favorites include *The Catcher in the Rye*, *The Adventures of Tom Sawyer*, and anything by Kurt Vonnegut — I can revisit these quickly; material I'm reading for the first time takes longer.

Here's what to do:

- Place your phone and all devices in a different room. Turn your notifications off. If you need to be reachable by your kids or school, or if you provide on-call services, adjust the settings so those calls can get through but silence all other notifications. (This will be true for just about every monotask in this book, so you're going to see this one repeatedly.)

- Choose reading material that appeals to you — rereading a favorite book from decades ago is fine, or it can be a magazine, a newspaper, whatever piques your interest. The act of reading and keeping your focus on the page is what's important at this point, not how intellectually challenging the content is. If it's been a long time since you have done any concentrated reading on paper, don't start out with *War and Peace* or a complicated medical journal if that's not your usual fare.

- Find a place to read that will be peaceful. You may need to get up a bit earlier or find a quiet spot on your lunch break, let family members or others know you need a break, or choose a time when your children are busy with an activity that isn't likely to require your attention.

- Bring your full attention to the book or magazine while you read.

- Try to read at the same time every day for a week so that it becomes a routine.

- If your mind wanders, bring your focus back to the pages, and be gentle on yourself. Your brain has gotten used to flitting from task to task, and you're essentially in the process of retraining it, not unlike training your muscles if you're taking up a new sport or activity.

- As you build the routine of daily reading, add more time to this monotask. Perhaps you can do fifteen minutes in the morning and thirty minutes at night, or whatever best accommodates your schedule.

- As you observe the benefits of reading, you will find the right balance of time. Like other good habits that can make you feel better, such as exercise, you will notice that daily reading has a calming effect and improves your ability to move through life with new effectiveness and focus.

- Realize that the benefits of monotasking accrue over time. Stay with it.

Your Mantra: "Just Read"

A mantra is a word or phrase that you repeat over and over again while performing a spiritual or physical practice. Mantras usually have a dual effect achieved through the power of the words you are saying and the repetition of those words, which may bring a trance-like state, or simply a focused mind.

Monotasking can be daunting; it can often feel like you are not doing enough if you are only doing one thing at a time. Here is where having a mantra for each monotask can be affirming—our mantra for reading is to repeat the phrase *Just read* over and over again in your head in order to focus on your primary task and let go of other distractions that come into your mind.

Whenever you find yourself distracted while reading, simply repeat the mantra in your head: *Just read*. Give yourself permission to monotask and focus only on the activity you are doing: reading.

Acknowledge that you are here at this moment to do one thing and one thing alone, and that is to read. Yes, you are capable of doing more. Yes, you have other things to do, but you will get to those later when it is their turn—now is the time to read.

Repeat it a few times if you need to: *Just read. Just read. Just read.* Tell yourself to bring your focus back to the book and only the book (or whatever you may be reading).

The Urge to Multitask

There are many distractions that will try to lure you away from reading. The key is to acknowledge them when they come to tempt you and then diligently return to your monotask. If you are experienced with meditation, this process of gently steering your attention back to your point of focus, without judgment, will be familiar.

If you have your phone, tablet, or computer nearby, there will always be an email that demands attention, a social media post to like, a game to play, a show to watch, a chore to do, a call to make, an errand to run, and so on. A study in the *Journal for the Association of Consumer Research* concluded that you don't even have to be using your phone for it to negatively affect your capabilities: "the mere presence of these devices reduces available cognitive capacity."

If you are reading on an electronic device, such as a Kindle or iPad, it is inherently a little more difficult to monotask reading than with a printed book. The temptation to be distracted looking up a word, switching to a different app, or multitasking while reading can be very strong. One option you may want to consider is to turn off the wi-fi on your device or put it in airplane mode while you are reading. It's not impossible to monotask while reading on a device, and certainly any reading is better than no reading, but I highly recommend the physical, tangible experience that comes from holding a book in your hands, feeling its weight and seeing where on the page you are.

You may drift into daydreams inspired by what you are reading or find that completely random ideas pop into your head. I go through life with a lot of Post-it Notes on hand. I stick them on just about every surface at home and in the office. When ideas come to mind that prevent me from staying focused on reading, I write them down, then feel confident I can let them go since they are documented somewhere.

When tempted to multitask while reading, be observant of whether your primary focus is still on reading. As for "background tasking" while reading, it can be performed in situations such as commuting on the train. In this scenario, reading is your primary task and "getting there" is your background task. Someone else is doing the job of getting you to your destination, and you can use your full attention to read (hopefully without missing your stop, as I have done before when immersed in a book!).

The Reinforcements

Like all habits, it can take time to make reading an integral part of your life. Strategies for reading success include:

- Read with others in your household. This may include reading at the same time with your partner or reading with your kids.
- Make a dedicated space for reading at home.
- Try new genres and discover what appeals to you so that reading is something you look forward to.
- Ask friends—or bookstore personnel or librarians—for recommendations. Sites such as goodreads.com are also helpful. Occasionally remind yourself of the advice of Haruki Murakami's character Nagasawa in *Norwegian Wood*: "If you only read the books that everyone else is reading, you can only think what everyone else is thinking."
- Read out loud. When you read to others, it requires more of your focus and it gives the words a third dimension. Some people absorb content more completely than

others while reading out loud; observe what works best for you.

- Join a book club, in person or online. Sometimes it helps to have group accountability or to be expected to talk about, ask, or answer questions about parts of the book.

- Wake up a little earlier and make reading first thing a part of your morning ritual, perhaps before you even get out of bed or interact with any devices. Many of us are tempted to reach for our phones as soon as we wake up, so instead try reaching for a book.

- Have a book with you wherever you go. Carry a book in the car or on your commute. There may be five or ten minutes of time throughout the day to read a chapter as you wait in a carpool line or for an appointment to start. (This sounds like multitasking, but "waiting" isn't a particularly demanding task, and pulling out a book to read can be more restful and fulfilling than mindlessly scrolling through your phone at these times.)

- Find a place where you enjoy reading outside your home, even if it's in your yard or on your porch. Perhaps it's at the library, a coffee shop, or in a park. It's amazing how sacred a simple spot can become when it is associated with regular reading for pleasure.

- Consider wearing earplugs or noise-canceling headphones while you read to help you stay focused on reading.

- Remember that you are never wasting time while you read. It's not always about the content or material you read. The simple act of reading, no matter what you read, focuses your attention and is valuable in and of itself. This is what monotasking is all about.

The Task in Your Past

Sometimes it is helpful to look to our past in order to build confidence and familiarity with a task to master it again. There was likely a time that each of us did some or all of the tasks in this book with complete focus. We are all fully capable, but we've gotten busy, we've become distracted, and we're constantly in a rush. You may find monotasks in this book where looking backward helps you connect with the inner monotasker from your youth; it does not have to be every task.

Was there a time in your past when you were a good reader? Perhaps when you were younger, when you were in school, or when you went through a training program for work? Even if there wasn't, that doesn't mean you can't learn to read effectively now.

Most people read a lot more when they were younger simply because reading was required for school assignments and because they had more spare time. When reading became optional and we could choose what activities to spend our time on, perhaps our reading consumption declined in favor of other media and hobbies. Looking back, if we were once a reader able to finish books in a matter of days or weeks, we can again rebuild the attention span and commitment to do so now.

One of my clients at Juniper Books loves having a collection of her favorite childhood books in her home. She doesn't read the books anymore, but she uses that bookshelf both to bring a smile to her face and remind her that she has been a lifetime reader. She has other contemporary books to read; those childhood volumes act as encouragement to sit down with her current reading list.

The great thing about reading as an adult is that we can make the conscious choice to do so for our own benefit and self-care. In most cases, no one is going to make you give a book report or force you to finish a book by a certain date. If we look at reading as a means to an end instead of an end in itself, and channel our lifetime experience as readers, we can hopefully find the time and motivation to improve our lives through a simple twenty minutes a day.

READING BY LISTENING

Sometimes reading a printed book isn't an option, which was the case for me for about a year after I had surgery for a hole in my head. I had been experiencing terrible headaches for more than a decade, and it turned out they were caused by a spinal fluid leak in the roof of my ethmoid sinus, essentially above my left eye.

What I hadn't realized before the surgery was how hard recovery was going to be — and that I wouldn't be able to read for a while. As a bookseller, that was something I would have liked to have been informed of in advance! The surgery left me with blurred vision in my left eye for months, and as the surgery was performed on my skull and very close to my brain, the pain in my head was intense.

I couldn't sleep well for most of that year. When I got home the first night, I put on an audiobook — *1776* by David McCullough. I ended up listening to thirty-five audiobooks in the months that followed. And not short ones — some took thirty to forty hours to complete! I would listen for hours and hours at a time.

Yes, I missed the act of reading on the page. But listening to books let me experience them another way — the only way I could — and I was able to sharpen my listening skills at the same time.

Some of my favorite audiobooks in recent years:

- *The Swerve* by Stephen Greenblatt
- *A World Lit Only by Fire* by William Manchester
- *Educated: A Memoir* by Tara Westover
- *A Brief History of Time* by Stephen Hawking
- *Leonardo da Vinci* by Walter Isaacson
- *In the Heart of the Sea* by Nathaniel Philbrick
- *SPQR* by Mary Beard
- *Alexander Hamilton* by Ronald Chernow
- *Beloved* by Toni Morrison (and read by Toni Morrison)

How You'll Know You're Good at It

Are you doing it right? First, there's no real "right"—but your goal is to be able to sit down and read for at least twenty minutes without mental or physical interruptions, and to absorb most, if not all, the information you read.

- You'll know you're good at it when your attention stays with what you are reading.
- Over time, it's a great goal to read more often and for longer periods of time. But remember that no matter how often or how long you read, the real measure of success when monotasking reading is that you can stay focused on the printed page.
- You'll know you're good at it if you look forward to reading different material and genres. If you always read self-improvement books or business books, try out a history or a biography. If you haven't read fiction in a while, give it a go and experience storytelling and

cultural immersion from new perspectives. As you move through bookstores or browse your library's website and gather recommendations from various sources, your expectations of what constitutes a good book may evolve. You may find books holding your interest that are unlike anything you've ever read.

- You'll also know you're good at it if you are a couple of chapters into a book and decide it's not the book for you. You are focused and you want to spend your time wisely. Once you regain your focus through reading, you will realize that spending ten or twenty hours on one book is worth your time only if the book is good — if it entertains you, if it exposes you to new ideas, if it teaches you something. Or if you simply enjoy it.

What if...

...*you're dyslexic or have trouble reading?* Try to find a substitute activity that brings your attention to one place and does not let it go. Audiobooks are an option, but make sure to monotask them; it's very easy for one's attention to wander while listening. (See sidebar "Reading by Listening," on page 38.)

...*reading while traveling makes you carsick? Or you've turned out the lights at home but still want to read?* Again, an audiobook may be the answer. Libraries offer audiobooks, and Audible and Apple Books have thousands of titles available for purchase. LibriVox and Libro.fm are also worth looking into for your audiobook searches.

...*reading just doesn't work for you?* We all will have monotasks that are easier or harder for us — it's okay to invest more energy into the other tasks if one does not work for you; they all provide benefits. Come back to reading periodically to give it more chances. Perhaps a better experience will be possible after you have strengthened your monotasking muscles.

Go Read!

At this point, I recommend putting this book down and picking up a magazine or another book and reading for at least twenty minutes. The key to reading and each of the monotasks is to do the task and nothing else. After a few starts and stops, you will likely find yourself in the groove without even realizing it.

Come back to *The Twelve Monotasks* after you have practiced your reading monotask with other material. Then reread this chapter to consolidate your monotasking skills. The act of rereading without getting bored or distracted takes an additional level of focus and commitment. Look for details and information you may have missed on the first pass.

When you feel like you have mastered this task, it's time to move on—you can always come back for a refresher. That is another great thing about books and reading: The words will still be here for you.

TASK 2: WALKING

I n 1845, Henry David Thoreau put down his iPhone and walked into the woods around Walden Pond.

Okay, I made that up. But imagine for a moment that Thoreau did have a smartphone and that all he had to do to leave the modern world behind in 1845 was to put it down and walk into the woods.

Thoreau was walking away from a life that seemed overwhelming, disconnected, and without purpose. He didn't live in the woods for two years and two months to get the perfect Instagram shot (#cabinlife) or even to write a best-selling book. In Thoreau's own words from *Walden*, this is why he left his "smartphone" behind:

> I went to the woods because I wished to live deliberately, to front only the essential facts of life, and see if I could not learn what it had to teach, and not, when I came to die, discover that I had not lived. I did not wish to live what was not life, living is so dear; nor did I wish to practice resignation, unless it was quite necessary. I wanted to live deep and suck out all the marrow of life...

Thoreau dispensed with everything but the essentials. He set aside the distractions and pressures of the world he lived in and monotasked his life in a way that few others will ever have the courage to attempt. Concord, Massachusetts, in the 1840s seems very peaceful and quaint to the twenty-first-century citizen; while I'm grateful for many aspects of modern life, I'm a bit envious of the slower pace of life back then, both in the village of Concord and especially on the shores of Walden Pond.

Thoreau's transcendentalist approach to life involved connecting with nature, slowing down, and being in the present moment. While in the woods, walking was an essential activity for Thoreau. In a later speech that was published as a book entitled *Walking*, Thoreau said, "I think that I cannot preserve my health and spirits, unless I spend four hours a day at least—and it is commonly more than that—sauntering through the woods and over the hills and fields, absolutely free from all worldly engagements."

Four hours a day walking. The monotask in this book is not *that* long, don't worry. But consider Thoreau, leaving his version of modern conveniences behind and walking for four hours daily. Does the thought of leaving your smartphone behind for five minutes terrify you? What about four hours...or two years?

I do not necessarily think that anyone needs four hours of daily walking, but Thoreau was onto something when he went into the woods to connect his body and his brain to the earth through his feet.

What if, like Thoreau, we walked for the sake of walking and nothing else?

For most of us, the act of walking itself is simple, but that's precisely the challenge. Simple tasks in our multitasking world can be among the hardest to do without giving in to the temptation of *doing something else at the same time.*

The Facts About Walking

We're walking more than we did in the past, which is great news. The Centers for Disease Control and Prevention reported that the percentage of adults in the United States walking for fun and exercise increased to more than 60 percent between 2005 and 2010. In a more recent pandemic-era study, Mintel found a big jump in walking and hiking among sixteen-to-twenty-four-year-olds in Great Britain.

While more people are walking, multitasking during the activity is also on the rise. I think anyone who has been out for a walk lately can attest to numerous instances of people walking with their heads looking down or having a conversation on their phones.

While the monotask of walking is not focused on getting in shape, the activity has substantial health benefits according to the Arthritis Foundation, including:

- Improved circulation, sleep, and mood
- Stronger bones, muscles, and joints
- Slower mental decline and lower risk of Alzheimer's
- Weight loss
- Longer and more active life

Walking is definitely a great monotask, benefitting both our bodies and our minds.

WALKING THROUGH CANCER

In life, we may have experiences where things are no longer available to us — a job, a relationship, or one of our senses or abilities due to injury or illness. These experiences can lead to concentrated focus and heightened sensations out of necessity, as it did for me.

Walking when I was going through chemotherapy taught me the simplicity of how to monotask my walks. I was very sick and weak a few months into chemo, but I was determined to get some exercise.

My walks were short on most days, but since we lived on a hill, they presented a challenge. First, I walked down the flat part of our street. At the point where the road tilted downhill steeply, I had to decide if I would have enough energy to make it back up the street and home. There were many days when I determined that it was too much to go down and then back up our hill.

Walking was truly all I could do for physical exercise for several weeks. Out on my walks, I had to focus all my physical and mental energy on walking and being able to get home.

To this day, when I go out for longer and longer walks, I appreciate every moment and frequently remind myself not to do anything but walk. Sometimes I'm tempted to look at my phone, take a picture, or make a call. But I try to gently bring myself back to the walk and enjoy it. I appreciate being alive and being able to walk and hike longer distances now. Everything else can wait.

Why Monotasking Walking Will Help You Do Everything Better

Any walk you go on is clearly good for you physically, but why is *monotasking* walking even better for you? The answer is that if you can focus while you walk, you can build a new connection between your body and your mind, and between yourself and the earth.

Walking is not a complex activity—for the most part, we can move our bodies on autopilot and at a reasonable pace without significant exertion. Our legs pretty much know what to do and that frees up our minds to focus on other areas. This combination allows us to strengthen our attention by monotasking walking, and then carry it through to other parts of our lives, especially other physical activities.

My friend Philip McKernan is a busy author, speaker, and coach. He is always well prepared for the retreats and events he hosts, so I asked him how he gets ready and received a surprising answer. I was expecting to hear that he spent the hours leading up to an event at a computer but, instead, he told me that he goes for a walk. He goes out into nature, without headphones, and gives himself space and time to walk. Taking a walk when we are busy and have a lot to do may seem like wasted time, but it is actually time very well spent.

Walking—just walking—can clear your head and help you reconnect with nature and the world around us. If we open our senses to the full experience of walking, we can see, hear, and smell a lot in a very short time.

 ## YOUR **WALKING** MONOTASK

Take a Twenty-Minute Walk

To do our walking monotask, we're going to isolate walking on its own. Not for exercise. Not to get from point A to B. Not to walk the dog. Not to multitask with a phone call.

Find twenty minutes in your day to set aside for your walk — as always, if you can't find twenty minutes or aren't yet able to walk for that long, *do what you can*. Remember that ten minutes is better than no minutes — it won't give you the full walking monotasking experience, but it's a start.

- Walk alone if possible. If you don't feel safe walking alone, enlist a friend who will agree to walk near you without talking. See the "What if..." section near the end of this chapter for more ideas on how to monotask walking in challenging scenarios.

- Choose a route where preferably you won't be interrupted or run into anyone you know.

- If you pass people, just give them a nod or a wave; don't stop to chat.

- Put your phone on Do Not Disturb, or ideally leave it behind if you feel safe without it.

- Do not listen to music, a podcast, or anything else.

- Do not take any pictures or videos. If a thought or problem comes to mind, let it go. Try to focus your mind on these sensations:

  - *Your feet.* Feel your feet. Relax your arches. Then do it again. It's helpful to remind ourselves to release tension in places where it tends to accumulate, such as our feet.

  - *Sounds.* Listen to the sounds that surround you, whether they are natural or the man-made environment. Listen to the sounds that you make walking.

  - *Your body.* Relax your shoulders and your neck. Think about how you carry yourself through space and try to be more relaxed about it. Let your body find its place and natural movement.

- *Connection.* Try to connect your body and its movements with the air and the earth. Your ancestors did this — they walked all the time. Connect with the long history of people moving while connected to our planet by walking.

After your walk, if you like, write down your observations of what you saw, smelled, and heard while walking. Note how you felt. Were you distracted? Engaged? Tired?

Try to take a twenty-minute monotasking walk at least one day a week and give it your full focus. Notice how the water runs down the street into the gutter, how the birds are coming back in the spring, how drivers are or are not paying attention. Take it all in. Sometimes you will notice houses or other things on your walk that you have passed thousands of times but never noticed, because your mind was elsewhere.

For some people, it will be challenging to find the time to walk; for others it will be difficult to monotask their walks. Can you truly commit to walking on its own? Can you pause thinking about work, life, and your to-do list while you walk? Are you able to not take your phone out of your pocket? Can you be content with the soundtrack of your environment?

Let go of the notion that you're walking to get exercise or you're walking to get work done at the same time. This is not about efficiency. You are walking to reclaim your attention.

Your Mantra: "Right Foot, Left Foot"

Repeat the mantra *Right foot, left foot* as you walk.

Focus on your movement and the balance between right and left, the rhythm of one-two, one-two, the cadence of each leg swinging and striking. With the help of the mantra, walking becomes something anyone can focus on and make progress.

Observe when you get bored or start thinking about work or some other aspect of life, and when that happens, simply return to your mantra.

The Urge to Multitask

You might be completely bored while walking and ask yourself if you shouldn't be doing something with this time, like making a phone call. Or answering a text, or checking social media. Try to stick with walking on its own and resist the temptation to combine it with another activity.

We may sometimes feel like walking is wasted time unless we are doing something else simultaneously. Tasks that are routine to us often feel as if they are prime multitasking opportunities. For example, if you follow the same walk to work every day and you've mastered it, then perhaps it seems like you should layer on some productivity. While you explore and practice monotasking, try to avoid layering any additional tasks onto your walk.

Should you be walking faster, or maybe go for a run instead to get in shape? Think of walking as an end in itself, not something you do until you are in shape enough to run.

Should you be using the time to catch up with a friend? Walking is a wonderful way to catch up with friends, so definitely do that, but also make time to take walks by yourself. It may be uncomfortable at first, but solo walking has tremendous benefits in times when we are rarely alone or in silence.

The Reinforcements

Throughout this book, we'll get creative using different reinforcements for different tasks. There are reinforcements that are good for all tasks, such as announcing your intention publicly. For example, for this task you could write a note and post it on your refrigerator: "Go for a walk!"

Then there are reinforcements that are very specific to each task. The key with monotasking is to find the subtle reinforcements that can better establish an effective habit, but not be so rigid about it that they become self-defeating. Here are some reinforcements specific to walking:

- *Be prepared.* Wear comfortable shoes and dress for the weather. Our minds can easily be derailed from monotasking if a physical need commands our attention. Being prepared will help you stay focused while you walk and not get distracted by any discomfort. Bring a water bottle and a snack. Make it a point to get out for a monotasking walk no matter what, even when the weather isn't great.

- *Routine.* When it comes to walking, I find that having a routine really helps. Creating a weekly schedule where you set aside certain times and days for a walk is ideal.

- *Setting.* Calm, quiet areas are a real blessing for monotasking walks. Taking a walk that doesn't require transportation maximizes your walking time; however, walking somewhere you are not familiar with also has a lot of value because you'll see many new things and may be able to find a more peaceful setting. If you live in an urban environment, you might want to take a short ride away to walk in an area that has fewer distractions.

- *Observe.* You may enjoy keeping track of new things you observe on your walk—you can journal about them after your walk if you like. Such as when you notice something you've never seen, or when you hear your footsteps in the silence of the forest for the first time.
- *Enjoy.* Feel the joy and contentment that comes from walking, in this moment, in the now.
- *Reward.* Maybe at the end of your walk, stop for coffee or a treat. This shouldn't be your goal at the end of every walk, but definitely treat yourself from time to time.

The Task in Your Past

Learning to walk is one of the most formative experiences for all of us. It's our ticket to exploring our surroundings. Before walking, we're on the floor, we're in our parents' arms, or where people want us to be. After we learn to walk, it's a whole new world.

If you can, look at baby pictures and connect to that sense of pure joy when you got up off the floor and were able to be mobile. It was wobbly and uncertain, and likely struck fear in the hearts of our parents and caretakers to see us on the move—new hazards appeared all of a sudden everywhere we walked; thankfully, that did not last forever!

If you can connect to the mobility that you achieved at a young age, try to align your thinking with who you were then and who you are now. In between learning to walk and now, a lot has happened. But we can get back to the pure joy, exploration, wonder, and experience of the world that we once had when we first moved about on our feet.

Dedicated Walkers

Walkers are thinkers and creators; thinkers and creators are walkers. Aristotle was one of the most influential thinkers and he walked frequently on his own and with his students—it was a way for them to creatively engage. Modern-day walking enthusiasts include Madonna, Kate Hudson, and Natalie Portman.

Jean-Jacques Rousseau was born in Switzerland—a country that to this day is one of the finest places to walk given its walking culture, an abundance of beautiful trails, and scenic views. In 1732, Rousseau wrote, "Walking animates and enlivens my spirits; I can hardly think when in a state of inactivity; my body must be exercised to make my judgment active. The view of a fine country, a succession of agreeable prospects, a free air, a good appetite, and the health I gain by walking; the freedom of inns, and the distance from everything that can make me recollect the dependence of my situation, conspire to free my soul, and give boldness to my thoughts, throwing me, in a manner, into the immensity of beings, where I combine, choose, and appropriate them to my fancy, without constraint or fear."

WALKING WHERE YOU ARE

I grew up in New York City and prefer walking the streets to just about every other mode of transportation. It's a wonderful way to experience what's really happening on the ground wherever you go, even a place you are already familiar with. I love exploring downtown New York City by foot, especially SoHo. New York is full of distractions — loud noises, weird smells, and you have to stay alert to traffic and passersby. It's not necessarily relaxing compared to other places I love to walk but I still find joy in it.

When I went off to college in New Hampshire, I immersed myself in outdoor activities, including hiking, that I had very little experience with growing up in

New York City. I remember when I came back from school and spent time in upstate New York, I discovered there was a nature preserve across the street from the house where I learned to walk as a toddler. Until then, I didn't know it was there! Now when I visit, I love to explore the winding trails through the woods and alongside natural ponds. The woods are peaceful and quiet, filled only with the sounds of frogs, birds, and other creatures.

Where I live now in Colorado, I'm very fortunate that there is a strong community dedication to preserving open space. These areas are protected from development and usually have walking and biking trails for recreational use. I'm grateful to be able to walk right out my door and choose either a short walk to the south or a longer loop to the west. Within a couple hours' drive, there are hundreds of trails to explore of varying difficulty, and an infinite number of beautiful things to see.

Wherever you grew up, wherever you live now, and wherever you visit, there is always a place to walk. It may take a little work to find or rediscover where to walk and set yourself up for monotasking success. The effort is worth it.

How You'll Know You're Good at It

I'm not a fan of clichés, but the saying "you have to learn to walk before you can run" seems appropriate here. You do have to learn the basics of something before performing the advanced version of that task. Whether you run — literally run — is up to you, but I'm confident that you will run with newfound focus when you do so! Speed is not the overall goal; the criteria listed here are a better indicator of your mastery of the task. You'll know you are good at monotasking walking when:

- You walk without feeling the need to do other things at the same time.
- You can decide consciously whether to add thinking, photography, or conversation to your walking.
- You look forward to your walks.
- You make time when you are busy, *especially* when you are busy, to walk.
- You aren't in a rush when you walk, and you may not have a destination.
- You are comfortable walking by yourself.
- You are comfortable turning your phone off, or at least in your pocket on Do Not Disturb.
- You notice different things on your walks, perhaps in an area you've been dozens or hundreds of times before.

What if...

...you have limited mobility due to physical limitation? Our goal is monotasking easy movement—the idea is to practice a form of movement that does not require a lot of brainpower, has minimal risk of injury, and allows you to focus while you do it. Other possible activities to practice this monotask include riding a stationary bike, doing gentle underwater exercises, using a rowing machine, practicing Tai Chi or Qigong.

...you can't leave your kids? If your kids are at an age where they can ride in a stroller or you can carry them on your chest or your back, take them with you. I remember those days—the kids either fell asleep, chatted about what they saw, or cried and then we returned home for a snack or a diaper change. Oftentimes, the walk resumed indoors and creative stroller laps lulled them to sleep.

…you prefer to hike? Go for it and apply all the principles of monotasking to your hikes. I have used the term "walking" in this chapter to make it accessible to more people, but if you are able to hike comfortably on a regular basis, feel free to substitute hiking for walking anytime you want.

…you can't go outside because of weather, air quality, darkness, or safety concerns? Some issues can be addressed by having the right clothing, footwear, and reflective garments. Other concerns are not so easily overcome. When we take a monotasking approach to our walks, including the preparation that happens before we put our shoes on or go outside, we can come up with creative solutions. Walking inside is one option—plan a route through your home, walk in the hallways or stairwells where you live or work, or use the space of a nearby mall or shopping center to walk. Safety concerns may be overcome by walking with friends, taking daytime walks on your day off, or taking a trip to a well-populated and brightly lit destination. Many of these approaches will create distractions of their own but that will encourage you to elevate your monotasking.

…you're on your feet all day and want to take a rest? Monotasking walking should be rejuvenating for your body and mind—it should not add to your exhaustion or feel like a chore. Try to go for a walk before or after work with this mindset. If walking still wears you out, save your monotasking walks for a day off.

Go Walk!

Go for a walk right now if you can. Feel the wind or sun on your face. Observe what you see, hear, and smell.

Come back invigorated and with a clear mind and ready to tackle whatever lies ahead.

Have a great walk! I'm heading out for one right now with my dog, Maple!

TASK 3: LISTENING

Quick question—who is the best listener in your life?
Don't think too long about it. Just blurt out who comes to mind.

For some of us, the best listener may be someone who gets paid to listen to us, such as a therapist, coach, or adviser. They listen for a living and have a lot of experience with it.

For others, maybe we've lucked out and our best listener is a parent or romantic partner.

Most people I ask this question answer that a friend is their best listener—someone who is neither a professional nor a relative.

Good listeners tend to be uncommon. We probably have a lot more friends and family who are *not* good listeners. Why is listening so hard? Has it become more difficult to listen as the world gets noisier? Do we have too many other things to do that we're too distracted or busy to listen?

My criteria for determining who is a good listener is a combination of factors:

- Someone who takes the time to listen and isn't in a rush. Time slows down for both of us when true listening happens.

- Someone who isn't constantly judging what I'm saying or how I'm saying it.
- Someone who isn't too quick to dispense advice—but, instead, feels out whether I'm looking for advice or just someone to listen.
- Someone who doesn't interrupt when I'm speaking or talk over me.
- Someone who acknowledges what I've said and demonstrates they have been listening.
- Someone who, when it's their turn to speak, doesn't start a monologue but instead engages in a two-way conversation; I listen to them just as they listened to me.

We all know a lot of people who are not so good at these things— that friend or relative who talks nonstop to the extent that you can't get a word in edgewise, or the coworker or client who seems so distant that you know they are multitasking, reading emails, or doing other work while supposedly in conversation with you.

And probably we're also guilty of those things from time to time.

We all want to be heard, and listening is where it starts. It can be frustrating when you are a good listener and others are not, but the more you model it, the more likely others are to follow. When we mono-task listening, we can achieve substantially more in our lives. We can truly hear what people are saying, we can be empathetic, and we can even do a better job listening to ourselves. These improvements can all lead to stronger personal relationships and more success in our lives.

Our goal with this monotask is *not* to go to the Listening World Championships, if there were such a thing. As with reading and all of the other monotasks in this book, we want to learn how to pay attention to one thing at a time. With listening, monotasking can pay huge dividends immediately, not only for listening itself but for many other things in life.

You'll hear more, learn more, understand more, and perhaps empathize more. Listening to your friends, a partner, coworkers, and family could make you the best listener they know, and how great would that be if they would give your name in answer to the question I asked at the beginning of this chapter: Who is the best listener in your life? For me, that would be like winning the Listening World Championships.

The Facts About Listening

It seems as if our world is becoming increasingly noisy and it's difficult to genuinely listen to one thing at a time. Websites, TV, and streaming services deliver an endless flow of content. Advertisers are constantly trying to get our attention, often with catchy jingles and loud commercials; our phone notifications make all sorts of sounds; and sometimes there are multiple people in our lives trying to get our attention at the same time. Since just about everyone is going through a similar experience, it has become somewhat acceptable to be distracted—everyone is and knows what that's like—but not being listened to can still hurt.

Have we become bad listeners or have we always been this way? Is there a limitation in the human brain that makes listening difficult or a more advanced skill than others? A *Harvard Business Review* article from 1957—before the modern technological age—explained one reason why we may not be good listeners: There's a disconnect between the rate at which we talk (about 125 words per minute) and the faster rate at which our brains process information. The authors, Ralph G. Nichols and Leonard A. Stevens, stated: "When we listen . . . we continue thinking at high speed while the spoken words arrive at low speed."

They went on to say, "In the act of listening, the differential between thinking and speaking rates means that our brain works with hundreds of words in addition to those that we hear, assembling thoughts other than those spoken to us. To phrase it another way, we can listen and still have some spare time for thinking."

To put it in multitasking and monotasking terms: Our brains might be multitasking because they seemingly have the capability to listen *and* to do something else at the same time. However, just because we *can* multitask in certain situations, does not mean that we *should*. (If you're monotasking this book, you'll notice that I repeat this statement in different places—it is an important point to remember.)

Yes, we have the ability to nod our heads while a friend is talking and check our texts at the same time. But do we have the cognitive function to truly hear what our friend is saying and to take in the text we are reading and responding to at the same time? Maybe for low-stakes conversations and inconsequential texts we can, but that tricks us into thinking we can do it anytime we need to. It's not possible to multitask effectively when we're listening to people tell us about troubled relationships, fears over current events, or other big life moments. Listening deserves our full attention, as do the texts when it's time to focus on them.

The challenge of being a good listener is not a new problem, but technology makes it easier to cover it up. We can be on the phone or in a meeting, and keep up just enough, saying the right thing at the right time, while being engaged in something else on our devices.

We can do better.

||||||||||||||||||||||||||||||||||||||||||||||||||||||||||||||||||||||||||||||||||||||||||||||||||||||

LISTENING TO CONNECT AND ENJOY

After my divorce, I started dating for the first time in nearly twenty years. The first date I went on was at a Starbucks. There was no chemistry, which was obvious from the moment we said hello. But we had a nice cup of tea and went our separate ways. I kept going on dates and pretty much had the same experience over and over again. No chemistry, nice conversation, two people talking, but not, necessarily, with each other.

Friends had considered me to be a pretty good listener over the years, but I observed when it came to my new-found dating life that I had a hard time listening and being present in many of the conversations. I was distracted. I was thinking about the past, the future, and a million other things. With each disappointing date, I was also worrying about whether I was ever going to meet someone I really liked and whether this was a waste of time.

Why wasn't I listening? Was there too much going on in my life? Was I not trying hard enough?

After about a dozen first dates where we didn't click, I went out with a woman I was very attracted to and very interested in. But the same thing happened as before. Essentially each of us took turns talking about the end of our previous relationship and neither of us actually listened to the other.

Had I lost the ability to focus during a conversation and hear what the other person was saying?

What if I focused on *listening* in these conversations? Not on talking. Not on overthinking whether I was attracted to the person across the table or trying to solve their problems or have them solve mine. When it came to dating, I resolved that even if I wasn't going to meet my soul mate on these dates, at least I could be a better listener.

It turns out that everyone has a lot to say and we all want to be heard. One result of paying attention more closely was that I had a good time on almost every date even if there was no chemistry. Simply putting a bigger effort into listening made nearly every experience enjoyable, or at the very least, interesting. I was treated to fascinating stories, I learned about humanity, and I eventually met people I wanted to spend more time with. I also heard a lot of what I may have been missing but was really always there.

‖‖‖

Why Monotasking Listening Will Help You Do Everything Better

The benefits of being a good listener include gaining respect and trust, boosting confidence, making fewer mistakes, developing patience, learning something, improving relationships, increasing empathy, becoming more popular, gaining understanding, having shorter work meetings — and getting good advice. That's quite a long list!

One great thing about listening is that you have a lot of opportunities every day to practice. Another great thing about listening is that the better you get at it, the better you will be able to control your attention and apply it where you want.

Listening is definitely a skill that needs to be developed. We live in a world where everyone seems to want us to listen to them, or at least look in their direction when they make some noise. Some want us to listen because they truly care about us and want us to care about them. Others simply want to monetize our attention by selling more ads, products, and services. The key is being able to distinguish between your listening opportunities and to choose wisely where you should focus.

YOUR **LISTENING** MONOTASK

Hear Every Word and Every Silence

We're going to start with twenty minutes of focused listening as our monotask. This may seem like a little or a lot depending on your perspective, but studies have shown that many people have a hard time paying attention for longer than twenty minutes, so that is where we will begin.

Our goal is to build our monotasking muscles so that twenty minutes of dedicated listening — or other tasks — does not seem difficult. For this monotask, we're going to practice listening in two different formats: "one-way listening" (to a recording) and "two-way listening" (a conversation).

Both of these tasks strengthen our ability to focus and pay attention while we listen. Listening to a recording, or what I'm calling one-way listening, is more forgiving, as you can replay a clip multiple times and there are no hurt feelings if you don't absorb all of the information. That being said, it can still be a challenge to pay attention, not tune out the recording, and stay focused in your first attempt at listening.

Having a conversation with another person and truly listening is one of the most important skills that we can possess in our lives. However, what I'm referring to as two-way listening is often taken for granted as something we instinctively know how to do. Two-way listening can be more challenging and complicated than we give it credit for. Listening with our full focus is a skill worth practicing at every possible opportunity.

Monotask 1: One-way listening

- Put your phone on Do Not Disturb and turn off the notifications. If you are not playing audio from it for this exercise, consider turning your phone off and putting it in another room.

- Find a quiet place to be undisturbed for twenty minutes.

- Choose something to listen to, such as a podcast, an audiobook, or a lecture (not music) that is at least twenty minutes long. While we may be used to background tasking these types of recordings in our lives, this time we are going to make listening to this type of recording our primary task. Put another way, don't put on a podcast while cooking — put on a podcast, sit down, and listen to it with intense concentration!

- I like to wear over-the-ear headphones when I'm really trying to listen well and minimize distractions.

- Settle back and listen.

- If you find your mind wandering, gently steer it back to what you're listening to. This is a similar strategy to how we approached the monotask of reading.

- When you're done, ask yourself questions about what you listened to; perhaps jot down the main points.

- Play what you listened to one more time and see how accurate your listening was.

Monotask 2: Two-way listening

For this two-way conversation you'll need to enlist the aid of a friend or family member — you can do this in person, over a phone call, or via FaceTime or some other app.

- Find a quiet spot to talk with as few distractions as possible — no television or music in the background!

- Explain what you're trying to do and that you want to practice your listening skills.

- Have some conversation prompts ready if needed. Ask about the person's family. Ask about their work. Or discuss something that you are both familiar with — an article you read, a podcast or something you heard on the radio, or maybe a trip you took together. It's best to avoid controversial topics during this exercise. For some people, a heated conversation may intensify the listening experience, but for others it may be distracting. If you end up in a heated conversation, observe how it impacts your ability to listen.

- Try to have a conversation as you typically would, but with extra effort put into being fully present and minimizing distractions and interruptions.

- When the other person speaks, you may be thinking ahead to what you are going to say in response, and this mental train of thought can override your listening. When this happens, gently bring yourself back to listening and paying attention to what the other person is saying.

- Be careful not to interrupt or speak over the other person — for some of us this may have become a habit we aren't even aware of. If the other person interrupts you, gently suggest that both of you practice a new approach to conversation where you each have a chance to finish speaking.

- Try to be aware of the rhythm of the conversation, the back and forth, if you are both talking, and who is talking more.

- At the end of the conversation, or multiple times while you talk, take turns playing back what you hear the other person say. Say something along the lines of: "Here's what I think I heard you say about ___, did I hear that correctly?" By doing this, you can confirm what you heard, and the other person receives confirmation that you are listening.

The first time you try listening in this two-way conversation monotask, it may seem awkward to pay *so* much attention to a task you do every day without thinking about it. The process may allow you to discover some things you need to work on or be aware of — you may have to fight the urge to interrupt or correct the person mid-sentence. If your friend is willing, ask how they felt at the end of the conversation and if they felt heard; ask if you talked over them or spoke too loudly or softly.

As you return to monotask listening in additional conversations, add on the following when you feel ready:

- Pay attention to the intonation of the conversation. Are your voices going up and down? Can you pick up on words/phrases that are being emphasized in a different way?

- Can you tell if the other person is truly listening to you? Can they feel that you are listening to them? Do they lean in? Do they ask questions?

- Is your mind wandering? Can you focus on listening, even if you are not interested in the story the person is telling? Or if you don't agree, can you just listen?

- If the person stopped abruptly and asked you to repeat back everything they just said or the gist of it, could you?

The first conversation you have where you truly paid attention the whole time, no one may notice but you. Let this be your own personal moment of satisfaction and know that you're on your way to becoming a good listener whom people will appreciate, whether they are aware of it or not.

Your Mantra: "Listen Closely"

Here's where we get to listen to ourselves and see if we can really pay full attention.

Oftentimes, a mantra seems to disappear after you repeat it many times—you no longer hear it and the repetition becomes second nature. We're aiming for something different here: This mantra doesn't have to be repeated over and over. Say it just one time to remind yourself to listen closely.

Listen closely.

Say it to yourself while in conversation with others. Say it when you're listening to a podcast or audiobook and you've drifted off. Say it to yourself when you're in class or at work.

Tune in, like a radio. You have good reception. If you're not interested in the material, or you're in an exceptionally distracting environment, lean in and listen even more closely. These are great challenges, but they are also real life—we can practice listening regardless of who or what we are listening to.

The Urge to Multitask

One of my friends has an uncanny ability for knowing when I'm doing something else while talking on the phone. She knows the instant I have checked out and calls me out on it. Why is she so good at sensing this? I think it's because she is a really good listener herself. I appreciate how attentive she is, and I make an extra effort now to give the conversation my full attention. Listening closely to her helps strengthen our friendship and it helps me practice being a good listener for others.

On the other hand, when I'm on the phone with a particular family member, I can check my emails and answer them the whole time. Is this because I'm a good multitasker? Absolutely not! I think it's because this person isn't the greatest listener. They rarely pause for me to speak. Even though these interactions are often one-way conversations, I shouldn't consider this to be permission to multi-task while on the phone.

But let's face it: It's so easy to pretend to be present and think about something else or actually do something else while ostensibly listening. Our phones and other technology make it easy to multi-task while listening—and they lull us into believing we are good at it.

When we nod our head in conversation and simultaneously engage in texting someone else, we likely feel validated that we're good at multitasking if our friend keeps talking and the person we are texting with replies. This makes us think we are successfully doing both things well, so we keep doing it. Maybe we check emails or carry on a Snapchat conversation while listening to lectures at school. If our grades don't suffer too much and our friends keep chatting, then we keep doing it. The way companies design apps and other user experiences these days constantly seems to affirm that we are doing a good job using what they offer, so we keep on using them and frequently multitasking in the process.

The Reinforcements

We are living in a world where people look at their phones constantly and where multitasking has become somewhat acceptable. Listening is one of the first things to suffer. Those who are focused appear to be more the exception than the rule.

So, how do we become better listeners? How do we be the ones who listen instead of accepting the status quo? Adam Bryant, author of *Quick and Nimble* and managing director of mentoring firm Merryck & Co., includes great suggestions in his article "Be a Better Listener" in *The New York Times*. These include being fully present, showing you're listening, and listening to learn. These are all great concepts for becoming a great listener, and they can also be applied to other monotasks and parts of our lives.

If you're reading the chapters in this book sequentially, by now you may have a good idea of ways to be fully present: Turn off and put away your phone, clear your mind and your schedule, sit in a comfortable place. Since listening is a monotask that often involves another live person, our presence is very important, not only for our ability to listen, but for the other person to feel heard.

Once we arrive in a conversation, we need to stay there with our attention. This can be very difficult in a world where it is expected that minds may wander and distractions will happen. Our body language should reflect that we are paying attention and truly listening. Look at the person you're speaking with and respond to what they are saying: this may be a smile or a nod or even leaning forward.

As you have a conversation, think about what you are learning. You're not in a conversation to do all the talking. Hopefully you are learning to become a better listener and you are learning about the other person. Instead of wanting to always share your experience or to instruct the other person in something, *see what you can learn.* Ask questions — or just give the other person room to talk.

All these things can help you become a better listener. See the monotasking.tips site for more ways to improve listening.

The Task in Your Past

Listening is a monotask that many of us probably didn't do so well as children. We may have only listened to our parents some of the time. Sitting still and listening at school is a perennial challenge for many.

On the other hand, it's important that we were *listened to* in our younger years. The National Children's Bureau in the United Kingdom reports, "Babies who are not listened to are likely to grow up with low self-esteem, while those who are listened to have a sense of well-being and are likely to be less anxious."

Think back to when, as a child, you really listened to someone and maybe they really listened to you. Perhaps you were captivated by their voice, their manner of speaking, or the story they told. It might have been a teacher or librarian reading a book aloud to the class or a parent or grandparent telling a bedtime story. Or maybe it was seeing a really cool scientific demonstration that captured your attention in a way that other subjects did not.

Back then, there wasn't quite as much circulating in our brains and competing for our attention. Depending on your age and how long ago it was, you may not have had a device and neither did anyone else around you. You probably didn't have a long list of things to do, bills to pay, or messages to send.

If we did things once, we can do them again. Listening is like riding a bicycle—even if you haven't done it in a while, you never forget how, and you'll be able to do it again. To get started, perhaps try to connect with someone or something you loved listening to in your younger years to refresh your feeling of being a good listener. Considering asking a family member to retell you a story you loved—chances are they'll be flattered that it had such an impact on you.

Dedicated Listeners

Indigenous peoples have long practiced the art of respectfully listening to others while they speak. Group conversations in many Native American communities take place in a circle, often with a "talking stick" or "talking feather" passed from one person to another as they take turns speaking. As quoted in *Indian Country Today*, John Peters of the Wampanoag Nation said of these practices, "The Talking Circle is...a listening circle. The talking circle allows one person to talk at a time for as long as they need to talk. So much can be gained by listening. Is it a coincidence that the Creator gave us one mouth and two ears?"

My friend Paola is a Spanish-language court interpreter, a job that requires intense focus and advanced listening skills. Besides being fluent in a second language, you have to be able to listen under pressure in a forum where people's lives and futures may be at stake. Decisions can be overturned based on the translation of a word or a phrase that can be interpreted differently, depending on the context and what country the speaker is from. Because the work is mentally exhausting—listening takes a lot of energy—interpreters work in teams and replace each other every twenty to thirty minutes.

Given the importance of listening and paying attention to the details in this job, and in many other fields—including medicine, mental health, education, and others—we should make sure we acknowledge the importance of listening skills to society and prioritize their development.

Stephen Covey, author of *The 7 Habits of Highly Effective People*, provides some of the clearest guidance for becoming a better listener in his fifth habit: "Seek first to understand, then to be understood." He explains, "Most people do not listen with the intent to understand; they listen with the intent to reply. They're either speaking or preparing to speak. They're filtering everything through their own paradigms, reading their autobiography into other people's lives." Covey goes on to discuss the concept of "empathetic listening," which he calls the "highest form of listening" and how by using it, we can truly understand those whom we interact with "emotionally as well as intellectually."

BACKGROUND LISTENING

I love my record player—it plays about twenty-three minutes on one side of a record, then it's over and you have to get up, flip the record to the other side, or put on a new one. When I'm listening to a record, I have a better awareness of the passage of time: I *have* to listen or I'll miss it. Twenty-three minutes flies by quickly.

While listening to a record requires at least some mono-tasking skills, streaming services like Spotify, Apple Music, and Pandora just keep going. This can lead to tuning them out and losing track of time. There is nothing wrong with background tasking your music listening; in fact, it can be very helpful and supportive to what you are doing as your primary task.

When I'm working on something that would benefit from music in the background, I try to choose music that promotes doing the primary task well. An obvious example is when I listen to loud upbeat music while working out. It gives me energy and makes the workouts more fun. I wish I could listen to music safely while biking, but given the prevalence of distracted driving, I want to be fully attentive and hear everything I possibly can while riding so close to cars on the road.

On the other hand, when I'm writing or doing some deep thought work, I either work in silence, or wear big over-the-ear headphones and listen to classical playlists on Spotify such as "Peaceful Piano," "Piano in the Background," or "Classical Focus." Other tasks I find are best accomplished while listening to different types of music, radio, or podcasts that provide the right mood and energy. Finding the ideal combination takes some experimentation and creativity, but that can be part of your overall listening monotask to find what goes well together.

There is no absolute rule against background tasking while building your monotasking muscles. In each situation where you might add a background task, try to bring some awareness to what is your primary task and what is your background task. If you can successfully pair your primary task to background listening that supports it, it can make you more productive and happier.

How You'll Know You're Good at It

Jillian Pransky, author and master yoga teacher, has developed a practice called "Deep Listening," which she says helps "cultivate the kind of conscious relaxation that allows you to stay open, present, and curious in situations where you normally wouldn't." These types of advanced listening skills are within reach of all of us, and can be achieved through dedication, a willingness to learn, and focus.

You'll know you're good at monotasking listening when:

- You practice deep listening
- You are AWOL less often. Mark Goulston, MD, professor of psychiatry and author of *Just Listen: Discover the Secret to Getting Through to Absolutely Anyone*, shared this advice with me: "Before you can listen, you have to be present. Don't go AWOL." AWOL of course is the military term for "absent without leave," but in this case he used it to mean "absent without listening." I love that simple concept. How many of us are AWOL in our daily conversations?
- You find joy in listening, in learning something new, and when you truly get what the other person is saying.
- You have fewer frustrating conversations where multitasking got in the way.
- Others become better listeners when they're with you. Good listening can be contagious.

What if...

...you're in conversation with:

- *someone you have a difficult relationship with?*
- *someone who gets angry at you or always wants to argue?*

- *a narcissist?*
- *an "enemy?"*
- *someone you simply can't stand?*

These are tricky situations that can require special skills or, in some cases, a friend or mediator to be present. You may need to just listen or take notes and not respond verbally at all. Sometimes two-way conversation is the source of a problem and just listening (not responding no matter how much we want to talk) is the best approach.

In some cases, you may need to stop having conversations with a particular person. While you are open to working on yourself, not everyone shares a similar mindset. If you've given it your best effort to listen and be listened to, and it doesn't work, it may be time to move on.

...despite your best efforts, you can't understand or remember the details of a conversation? Being present and an empathetic listener is of great value; you shouldn't devalue the type of listening you are good at. Take notes if the other person is okay with it, preferably on paper so you can stay more present in the conversation and not be distracted (or appear to be distracted) by your device.

...you have too much to do and really need to multitask while having conversations, otherwise you will fall behind? Do one thing at a time to do everything better! Try it—it works.

Go Listen!

Go listen, truly listen:

- to your partner
- to your kids
- to your pet (yes, your dog, cat, or other pet has a lot to say!)
- to your colleagues

- to an inspirational speaker
- to stand-up comedy, an interview, or a podcast
- to nature.

This may be one of the most challenging monotasks for some people, but it is also a monotask that we can practice frequently and ideally feel ourselves making progress with quickly.

TASK 4: SLEEPING

One of the monotasks that has the biggest impact on other monotasks is sleep. Without good sleep we're not able to operate at our best, and yet, when it comes right down to it, we typically do a lot more to stay awake than we do to get the sleep we need. We drink coffee, guzzle energy drinks, and often override our body's signals that we're exhausted. We pack our days so full that our to-do lists spill over into the nights.

The cultural landscape has historically been dotted with inventors, politicians, and many others who claim that a secret to their success has been their ability to work harder than everyone else and function on less than five hours of sleep per night. These superhuman men and women have built machines, created industries, and occupied the most powerful offices on the planet. Stories of the minimal sleep habits of extremely successful people include Thomas Edison in his Menlo Park laboratory and, more recently, Marissa Mayer, the former CEO of Yahoo!, saying she sometimes worked up to 130 hours per week. Margaret Thatcher served as prime minister of the United Kingdom reportedly on four hours of sleep per night.

Who could blame us for thinking that if the truly exceptional among us are able to pull off the miracle of minimum sleep and maximum performance, that we should strive for that, too? We want to keep up with the Joneses while we're awake. In order to find the time in our days to get more done, sleep is one logical place to borrow it from.

If I asked you how much sleep you *should* get a night according to medicine and science, I'm pretty sure I already know your answer.

Seven to eight hours.

We all know it, but we're not good at actually getting it. There are dozens of things that might distract us from giving sleep the attention it needs. One more episode of a show, another hour to work on an assignment, time to squeeze in a workout, they all can get in the way of sleep.

Because of insufficient sleep we leave the body and brain open to any number of maladies and ailments — obesity, diabetes, high blood pressure, heart disease, stroke, and mental health issues included. According to Matthew Walker, PhD, author of *Why We Sleep: Unlocking the Power of Sleep and Dreams*, "Sleep is the single most effective thing we can do to reset our brain and body health each day — Mother Nature's best effort yet at contra-death."

So, without further delay, let's focus on sleep while we're wide awake so that we can get better sleep later.

The Facts About Sleeping

Every human being has an advanced biological clock that regulates a number of processes in our body every twenty-four hours. The sun rises and sets, and that pattern drives our circadian rhythm. Our bodies have evolved to become tired at night and active and alert during the day.

Not getting enough sleep disrupts our circadian rhythm. Why we don't get enough sleep can include a multitude of reasons, some within our control, and others that we can't control — jet lag, working night shifts, sleep apnea, and other disorders among them.

Sleep deprivation is extremely common in America, and around the world. The CDC (Centers for Disease Control and Prevention) reported that 35 percent of adults are getting less than seven hours of sleep.

While we are sleeping less, our understanding of sleep and why our bodies need it has been improving. Matthew Walker explains, "Routinely sleeping less than six or seven hours a night demolishes your immune system, more than doubling your risk of cancer." Insufficient sleep can also contribute to memory loss (memories are consolidated in our brains during "deep sleep," part of a healthy sleep cycle), Alzheimer's, and cardiovascular problems.

Being tired also leads to poor performance. According to the AAA Foundation for Traffic Safety, more than 300,000 crashes occur every year from drowsy driving, and an estimated 5,000 people die from drowsy driving crashes.

The National Safety Council estimates more than 70 million Americans have trouble sleeping, and that an average employer with a thousand employees can expect to lose more than $1 million a year because of fatigue, with more than $500,000 in healthcare costs for those employees attributed to sleep issues.

As a society we should wake up (pun alert!) to the reality that some more sleep would do all of us good, and there is no shame in getting the sleep we need.

WHY AM I SO TIRED?

Two years after going through cancer treatment, I was completely exhausted. I tried everything to get over the fatigue — exercising, *not* exercising, seeing all sorts of doctors and alternative health practitioners, taking various supplements, changing my diet, and everything else I could think of. I knew that fatigue was a typical side effect of chemotherapy and that it could last for twelve or eighteen months, but I didn't think it would persist this long.

The fatigue manifested in strange, but ultimately predictable, ways. On a daily basis, I'd wake up with lots of energy, feel great in the mornings and have a very productive start to my days. Then, by 1:30 in the afternoon, I'd be hit with a wave of exhaustion — I could barely keep my eyes open, and I'd have to find somewhere quiet to lie down and take a twenty-minute nap right away.

After a couple years of this, I wondered if there was another reason that I was tired. Could it be that I simply wasn't getting enough sleep?

I thought I had pretty healthy sleep habits, going to bed early, waking up early, and generally feeling rested in the mornings. If you asked me at the time how much sleep I got, I'd guess that it was a solid eight hours a night. It turns out I was very wrong.

There are lots of apps and devices you can use to monitor your sleep. I tried out one called Whoop — it's a device that tracks various biometrics throughout the day and night and then provides a host of data and reports on your smartphone. The results really surprised me.

The first night I wore the Whoop strap — basically a watch that doesn't tell time — it told me that I had gotten four hours and forty-six minutes of sleep. The next night, five hours and one minute. Wow.

Now that I could measure my sleep and had some possible insight into why I was so tired, I set about getting more sleep. I wanted to get a solid seven hours — I didn't get there overnight (ha!) but I was able to make all sorts of adjustments and track them in the app, so over time I could see patterns.

Getting enough sleep on a daily basis is still a work in progress for me, but I've come a long way by monotasking my sleep.

Why Monotasking Sleeping Will Help You Do Everything Better

Like all the other monotasks in this book, sleep is something that can be isolated, worked on, and improved. Unlike the other tasks, you *have* to do this one every single day, and unless you do it well, there will be consequences.

When you do get enough sleep on a daily basis, your body can heal and prevent some illnesses. Getting enough sleep also improves our ability to pay attention, our cognitive skills, and our mood. Paying attention to sleep will help you pay attention to everything else in life.

 YOUR SLEEPING MONOTASK

Get more Sleep

Your sleeping monotask is going to yield major benefits. Be aware that this task is harder than it seems at first. It might take several nights, even several weeks or months, to see improvement. Don't worry if you're not progressing as quickly as you would like.

Patience is key. While the ultimate goal is to get *more* sleep, the initial purpose of this monotask is to bring our focus to sleep so that we can make changes and test if they work for us.

Note that children and teenagers need more than seven hours of sleep. I've set the goal at seven hours as a minimum for adult readers. If you already get this amount of sleep, you can follow the monotask to improve the *quality* of your sleep.

Sleep quality means that you fall asleep faster, wake up fewer times during the night, and get more deep sleep *and* REM (rapid eye movement) sleep. Deep sleep is when your body heals and consolidates memories; REM sleep is when you dream.

Getting ready for bed:
- Make a commitment to get at least seven hours of sleep.

- Set aside eight hours to be in bed (the extra hour is to account for the time it takes to fall asleep, and time awake in the middle of the night, even if you are not aware of it).

- Don't overthink the equation and don't resist the math. If you have to get up at seven a.m., you can't go to bed later than eleven p.m. (if seven hours of sleep is your goal). Further, if your body naturally wakes up at a certain time, don't fight it (at least not initially; you can try to gradually change that later) — subtract eight hours from the time your body wakes up, and be in bed at that time.

- Write down your sleep schedule and make it visible as a reminder to yourself — for example, "eleven p.m. bedtime, seven a.m. wake up."

- Turn all devices and the television off a minimum of thirty minutes before bedtime — the short-wavelength blue light from these devices can block the release of melatonin that signals your body it's time to sleep.

- Get in bed. Make your bed comfortable. Arrange your pillows exactly how you want them.

- Turn off all the lights and try to shut down or put away all light-emitting devices and electronics. Blackout shades are great for keeping outside light from getting in; eye masks are also helpful for many people. The darker it is, the deeper we can sleep.

- If you like sleeping with the windows open, open them before you get in bed. Studies have shown that cooler temperatures are better for sleeping. Try turning the thermostat down to sixty-five for the night.

- Make your bedroom as quiet as possible. If others in your home are staying up later than you, respectfully ask them not to have any loud conversations after your bedtime and to please wear headphones while watching shows or playing video games.

- If you know that you do better with some white noise or you find that it's *too* quiet to fall asleep, you can download apps, purchase a dedicated white noise machine, or play white noise from YouTube, Spotify, or Pandora. If you have never tried white noise as a sleep aid, it can't hurt to try it out and see if it helps you fall asleep and stay asleep.

- If your partner comes to bed later than you, request that they get their side of the bed and all their things ready twenty minutes *before* you go to bed. Then they can come into the room in the dark and not disturb you. If this is not workable, consider asking them to sleep in another room while you work on this monotask — yes, sleep is that important!

Now for sleeping itself:

- Let go of any thoughts from the day. If your mind is full of thoughts, set aside a few minutes before bedtime to write in a journal. Once the thoughts are down on paper, release them.

- Let go of any thoughts about all the things you need to do tomorrow. If you want to make sure you remember them, write up a to-do list before you get in bed.

- If, while falling asleep, some idea or urgent to-do item comes to mind, recognize that this is normal. Your brain is relaxing, and various things might rise to the surface. Ask yourself if these items can wait until the following morning — almost everything can indeed wait. Write down whatever came up and let it go.

- If you are having trouble falling asleep, read a few pages of a book or consider adding a pre-bedtime meditation practice. Both of these will bring your attention to one place and settle some of the busyness in your mind.

- If you wake up in the middle of the night, be gentle on yourself. Try to stay sleepy, keep the room dark, and don't reach for your phone. Doing so only stimulates your brain and puts you into multitasking mode, making it harder to fall back asleep. Taking a few deep breaths can help settle your body and mind, gently guiding you back to sleep.

- Wake up at your scheduled time. It's not necessarily bad if you are still tired when you wake up. When we wake up while in REM sleep, we can feel tired, but it does not necessarily mean that we didn't get enough sleep. We are also more likely to remember our dreams at this stage.

- Consider keeping a sleep journal next to your bed and write in it before you get out of bed in the morning. Note what time you went to bed, what time you got up, how you felt about your sleep, and any changes you made to your bedtime routine. It's helpful to look back at your notes and observe trends.

Your Mantra: "Sleep on Rails"

I like trains and the romance of traveling by train. When you travel by train, you can't go *wherever* you want to go; you have to stay on the train tracks (aka rails) and follow where they run.

When you don't have a choice of things to do or places to go, the decision to monotask is much easier. Therefore, I like to remind myself to *Sleep on rails*. Riding the rails (in the comfort of my own bed of course) from one point to another keeps me focused on sleep and prevents me from taking any side trips during the night.

The Urge to Multitask

What does your evening routine currently look like? When it's quiet and dark outside, you've had dinner, and you don't have to be anywhere for ten or twelve hours, do you enjoy the quiet time, or do you feel the need to always be doing something productive?

My natural inclination is to keep busy and try to be productive all the time. Years ago, I used to bring my laptop to bed just about every night and answer a few emails before falling asleep. I rationalized my nighttime attempts at productivity by applying Benjamin Franklin's aphorism, "Never leave that till tomorrow which you can do today."

While Ben's advice is usually sound, I would modify this one for the twenty-first century to read: "Don't put off until tomorrow what you can do today . . . except stop whatever you're doing one hour before bedtime and do whatever is left tomorrow."

Some people enjoy falling asleep on the couch with the TV on; others like to catch up on their social media at the end of the day. It can be hard to break the habit of doing these things before bedtime. They are enjoyable activities and you've earned the right to do them.

However, be aware that at a certain point, these activities impede your ability to fall asleep and get the quality sleep you need.

Set a firm timeline for when you will stop working, when you will disengage from social media and your devices overall, and when you will switch to sleep time. The clear separation will help you better enjoy everything you do. And you'll be less tired.

Here are some distractions that may tempt you away from mono-tasking your sleep. Be mindful of them and do your best to stay focused on getting the sleep you need:

- You need to "check one thing" on your phone.
- You remember something you need to do for work or school.
- Your thoughts are racing and you're feeling anxious.
- Your kids want your attention; they may be scared, lonely, or need help with something.
- You didn't get a workout in today, and there's still time to squeeze it in before bed.
- You're bored and maybe not that tired and think, why not go out for a drink? Your friends are out having fun, plus alcohol helps you fall asleep (note that while it may help you fall asleep, staying asleep and sleep quality are negatively impacted by alcohol).
- You're hungry and decide to eat right before going to bed.
- Red-eye flights may seem like a good idea for time management and doing more during the day, but they can wreak havoc on your sleep schedule.
- Night shifts — if they are unavoidable, try to follow the other sleep tips during the day.
- Sex at night — does it help you sleep or make it more difficult to fall asleep after?

We're human so some of these are going to get in the way of our sleep from time to time. Be compassionate with yourself—you may not be able to change your habits quickly. New habits can take weeks or months to stick. Plus, we may have to make exceptions every now and then.

Monotasking sleep will help you determine what works for you.

The Reinforcements

As you can see from the monotasking instructions on the preceding pages, monotasking sleep is not as simple as "Go to bed when you are tired, wake up when you are rested." If it were that simple, we'd all be getting the sleep we need, and we'd all be healthier, happier, and more productive. As Alex Soojung-Kim Pang puts it in *Rest: Why You Get More Done When You Work Less*, "Rest doesn't just magically appear when we need it."

Here are some reinforcements to help you get better sleep:

Wear yourself out. We naturally tire out after a long day of work (both paid and unpaid) and life. However, some people have more energy and need to exhaust themselves even further in order to get good sleep. Exercise is a great way to do this. Be aware, though, that exercising too close to bedtime can be overstimulating and make it harder to wind down. The ideal times for our body to exercise are in the morning or early afternoon. If you're not tired enough at bedtime, try for a little more exercise tomorrow during the day.

Clear your mind. Focus 100 percent on going to sleep when it's bedtime. Don't think about work, what happened earlier, or what you need to do tomorrow. Write things down if you need to in order to download them from your brain. No one can solve all their problems or do all their work at bedtime—when you try, you most likely are not doing your best work, and you are taking away from your sleep. All of us can benefit from a good night's sleep and then be better at doing our work and addressing our to-do lists the next day. Return to the sleep monotasking instructions from time to time for a refresher.

Minimize distractions and disturbances. When stressful situations arise at bedtime, it really takes a toll. If you get a disturbing text right before turning in, you may have trouble sleeping the whole night. Using social media at or near bedtime not only exposes you to the blue light that disrupts your melatonin production but increases the odds that you see something that "revs up" your brain and disturbs your sleep.

What we want to do is lower the odds of experiencing a distraction or disturbance as bedtime approaches. The best way to do this is to distance yourself from your phone for at least an hour before bedtime. I recommend *not* watching cable news, which seems designed to agitate us—this is not what you need before going to bed. By all means, stay informed, stay engaged, and pay attention to the news, but try to get your news from outlets that aim to inform you, not raise your blood pressure, and not right before bed.

Stay in the zone. I toss and turn a bit at night and typically wake up at least once. I make it a point to minimize how awake I become at these times. I keep my heart rate down and try not to get upset that I'm awake and losing sleep. I keep the lights as low as possible while making the trip to the bathroom.

Try not to "start your engine" in the middle of the night—don't pick up your phone (unless you need to put on white noise, a meditation app, or an audiobook). Don't start thinking about work or the problems of the day. The best thing you can do is to stay sleepy and go back to sleep quickly so that you can do what you need to do tomorrow.

Bring awareness to caffeine consumption. If you are a coffee drinker or other caffeine consumer, be aware that it can act as a stimulant for up to seven hours. If you go to bed at ten p.m., cut off your caffeine after three p.m. Giving it time to run through your system and not get in the way of your sleep requires some planning and discipline.

As you get more sleep on a daily basis, you may not need as much caffeine as you used to. Experiment with substituting tea for coffee, and herbal tea for caffeinated tea.

Make difficult changes. There may be some big obstacles between you and getting the sleep you need. We need to be honest about these and do what we need to do to stay healthy. Sleep is something we need every day and that is not going to go away. It's worth making the life changes and investments that will help you get more sleep.

It may be that you need to seek medical advice for a condition such as sleep apnea. Or perhaps you've made all the modifications you can think of to your bedroom, but if there's too much traffic noise or your roommates are noisy or there are other problems you can't work around, you may need to relocate. If you decide to move, visit new homes you are considering at night so that you can survey potential problems that would impact your sleep before making a decision.

You may need to have difficult conversations with your partner about what you need to get a good night's sleep. This may include sleeping in different rooms if snoring or tossing and turning is waking you up. It may also include agreements not to argue or discuss difficult topics before bedtime. You should also talk about sex and try to agree on what time of day is best for both of you to get more sleep—this doesn't sound that romantic but for a healthy, stable relationship, it's incredibly important.

Some relationships have irreconcilable sleep differences. If you cannot get the sleep you need, your relationship may not be happy. And if you are not happy, you will not get the sleep you need. It can be a vicious cycle. Try to work things out; see a couples' therapist if you can.

The Task in Your Past

When you were young, you probably didn't have to think about whether it was time to go to bed, or whether it was okay to fall asleep in the middle of the day for a nap—you just did it.

As adults, maybe we're embarrassed when we're tired during the day, can't stay up as late as others, or need more sleep than our friends and coworkers. If your situation allows, take a nap if you need one. I love short afternoon naps (lasting about fifteen to twenty minutes) and take one almost every day. Go home during the day or nap at your desk. At night, leave the party early or skip the work dinner. Your younger self wouldn't have waited for permission—you would have just fallen asleep when you were tired.

Your younger self also most likely was a miserable tyrant when you didn't get enough sleep. Perhaps you refused to sleep and the more tired you got, the more difficult you became. If you don't remember being like this, think of all the overtired children you've seen in public—you know what I'm talking about. The parents always say their child just needs a nap. Well, maybe you just need a nap, too!

Dedicated Sleepers!

In Washington Irving's famous 1819 short story, Rip Van Winkle takes a nap and wakes up twenty years later. I'd like to think that Rip was really tired and needed that twenty-year nap. Instead, it's one of the first examples of time travel in literature—Rip slept his way into the future. It's an intriguing idea to sleep *so long* that you wake up in a different world.

In Ottessa Moshfegh's *My Year of Rest and Relaxation*, published in 2018, the narrator medicates herself into a year of sleep. Readers are treated to an often hilarious and wild tale of prescription drugs and complex schemes pursued by the narrator in an effort to reset her life through sleep. One could argue that the protagonist is the ultimate sleep monotasker—she has one goal—to sleep—and she'll do anything to achieve it. However, her methods are extreme. While many of us can definitely relate to the main character's fatigue, it should be a cautionary tale in how *not* to pursue our sleep goals in real life!

Today, we're fortunate that sleep is increasingly being promoted as healthy and useful. Arianna Huffington wrote a book called *The Sleep Revolution*, which is full of excellent information and suggestions. She writes, "These two threads that run through our life— one pulling us into the world to achieve and make things happen, the other pulling us back from the world to nourish and replenish ourselves — can seem at odds, but in fact they reinforce each other." It's great to see that the idea of sleeping more in order to do more is getting its due.

PILLOW FORTS AND OTHER SLEEP TIPS

Monotasking my sleep has led me to come up with some strategies that never would have occurred to me otherwise. Here are some of the discoveries I have made about how I can get a good night's sleep.

- I can't sleep past 5:30 a.m. I wish I could sleep later, but I'm fully awake at this early hour regardless of when I go to sleep. Knowing this about myself helps me make sure I get enough sleep. There are only so many times I can stay up late and fall short of my goal.
- My mattress preferences change frequently. I'll go through phases when I prefer a firm mattress, other times a soft one. I purchased a Sleep Number mattress that allows me to change the firmness settings on my phone, and the two sides of the bed can be set differently. It was expensive, but the mattress has been a great investment for me since so much of life is spent in bed.
- I'm an adult and I sleep in a pillow fort! I sleep with four pillows — one under my knees, one on each side of me, and one under my head. I came up with this technique to lock my body in place while recovering from injuries, then I kept doing it as it

helps me truly sleep on rails. The pillows on my sides are the heavy variety and I find their weight very comforting through the night.

- I keep track of audiobook narrators with soothing voices. If I wake up in the middle of the night and can't fall back asleep, I sometimes put on an audiobook with one of these narrators. I won't mention their names as I'm not sure they'll take it as a compliment, but I appreciate their voices and how they make me fall asleep!

- I have a sleep window. If I go to bed around 9:30 p.m., I fall asleep *very* quickly and easily. If I stay up past ten p.m., it can take much longer for me to fall asleep. Only when I started monotasking sleep did I really recognize this pattern and then I adjusted my schedule and expectations accordingly.

- I take a fifteen-to-twenty-minute nap almost every afternoon. I love my naps and they recharge me for the second half of the day. It does take advance planning to be somewhere nap-friendly when you want to close your eyes. However, there should be no shame in knowing your needs and taking care of yourself by napping.

- I've learned the hard way to prioritize sleep when traveling. When I travel, I try to stay at a hotel or Airbnb close to where I need to be during the day so I can maximize sleep hours. I also ask for a room away from the elevator and high-traffic hallways. Traveling is exhausting on its own; I have to plan to get enough sleep and resist the temptation to overschedule myself.

How You'll Know You're Good at It

The first morning you wake up truly rested, you may be amazed—many of us don't realize that we have gotten used to functioning on a sleep deficit. You'll know you're good at monotasking sleeping when:

- You feel better throughout the day.
- You have more energy.
- You are able to do things you weren't previously able to do.
- You are able to focus more.
- Your mood improves.

Sometimes there will be disruptions or distractions—you won't get a good night's sleep every night. You'll know you are good at this monotask when you take the long view—when you don't get too worried about one night's sleep and you keep making adjustments to optimize your sleep over time.

I understand that if you have anxiety or panic attacks at bedtime, the last thing you might want to do is go to sleep—it can be a very disconcerting time for many. Try making a commitment to your sleep monotask during the day, then start your bedtime an hour or two earlier than your previous schedule. You'll know you are good at this monotask when you bring your attention to making changes to your sleep and sticking with the process.

Be aware that once you start sleeping more, your body may take days, weeks, or months before you feel fully rested. More sleep at first might actually make you feel more tired. This could be because you are getting more REM sleep and waking up during a REM cycle—this is a good thing and is healthy for your body. The extra sleep and tired feeling might also be your body recognizing that it now has the time to repair and heal you. You'll have to trust your body's ability to take care of itself while you sleep.

What if...

...you have sleep apnea or another condition that affects your sleep? There are definitely some conditions, such as sleep apnea and bipolar disorder, that get in the way of sleep and require medical treatment. There are sleep centers across the country now that can perform a sleep study in order to properly diagnose sleep disorders. Once you know what you are working with, you can monotask treatment and a new approach to sleep.

...you have long-term insomnia? Ask a doctor about supplements that may give you a gentle nudge—your doctor may recommend magnesium, cannabidiol (CBD), melatonin, 5-HTP (5-hydroxytryptophan, also known as oxitriptan, an amino acid), or taurine or theanine, also amino acids. In other cases, a prescription may be required. Be careful with prescription sleep medications as a long-term aid. Liz Cash, assistant professor at the University of Louisville, says, "Generally it is recommended that sleep medications be adopted only for the short-term, for four consecutive weeks of use or less."

...you have nighttime anxiety, night terrors, or nightmares? Many people experience difficulty falling asleep, or falling back to sleep when they wake up terrified, panicked, or disturbed. There is help—consult a therapist who specializes in this area.

Go to Sleep!

Really, it's your bedtime. Go to sleep.

Sleep on rails. See you tomorrow.

TASK 5: EATING

When I was growing up in the 1980s, my parents owned and operated a restaurant in New York City called the Quilted Giraffe. Reservations required weeks of advance planning, and on any given night, you might see Mick Jagger, Andy Warhol, or Madonna at a table. I worked just about every job in the house—coat checker, cashier, waiter, cook—it was a very fast-paced environment for the employees, but very calm and luxurious for the customers.

No one came with their phones (except the occasional customer with an early cell phone the size of a suitcase!). Children did not watch iPads during the meal. Nobody was posting food pics on Instagram. About the most high-tech feature in the restaurant was the wine list, updated and printed daily—a revolutionary achievement for the time.

Around the tables at the Quilted Giraffe, people savored their food and engaged in conversation. The primary distractions were waiters arriving to clear the table or pour more wine.

These days, it takes considerable effort to put away devices and focus on a meal. We might be eating by ourselves and like to have something to do. We might be having an adult conversation and want to keep the kids busy doing something else. It's not always this way in every household, but in the times we live in, it requires additional work and thought to have a dining experience that focuses on the food and the experience of eating.

At the same time devices and distractions have proliferated, the food world has evolved—it has never been easier to eat what you want without thinking much about it. A few decades ago, there were not many places to get a good burrito or gourmet pizza, and if you wanted a salad with twelve different ingredients, you had to make it yourself. Nowadays, there are fast casual restaurants everywhere and greatly expanded prepared foods sections in grocery stores. Fast food chains have expanded their menus, and all sorts of new food brands and products are squeezing onto the shelves of stores.

The rapid evolution in food and dining over the past few decades presents multitasking opportunities at every stage. Restaurants are frequently a source of sensory overload with large TV screens, open kitchens, and people-watching opportunities galore. When we sit down to eat at home, it's really easy to add another task, such as watching TV or reading. We can be so busy that we don't even bother to sit down or take our food out of its container.

The ease with which we now have access to food and eat our meals has unlocked time in our busy lives. But something is missing that can make our food taste better, our bodies healthier, our meals more enjoyable, our lives a little calmer, and our connections to friends and family stronger.

We can get back to it, one bite at a time.

The Facts About Eating

For most of history, humans were hunters and gatherers. Our days were focused on finding food, then sharing it and consuming it together. Perhaps some of the first multitasking occurred when stories were told around the fire while everyone ate!

Our ancestors knew where their food came from, and no doubt appreciated it as the sustenance that gave them life. Today, many people are less aware of the source of what we eat and the rush to consume meals and get back to something else is most likely familiar to all.

According to the Bureau of Labor Statistics, the average American spends sixty-eight minutes per weekday eating and drinking, which increases on weekends to seventy-six minutes. Some children at school have less than fifteen minutes to eat after they've stood in line to get their food. Depending on your perspective, this may seem like ample time, or feel like a rush to get food in our mouths before we move on to something else.

When Silicon Valley and venture capitalists look at where we spend our time each day, some see big opportunities in reducing the amount of time we spend eating even further. According to an article in *The Guardian*, meal replacement companies like Soylent were started because the founder thought food was an outdated concept: "chewing took too much time and kitchens were terrifying."

Consider the growth of the energy bar market. Up until the late 1980s, energy bars barely existed and where they did, had an unappealing texture and taste. Now, tasty energy bars can provide a quick breakfast, lunch, snack, or maybe even dinner. They occupy nearly a full aisle at every grocery store, and according to "The Energy Bar Market Report 2020," in 2019 the global energy bar market was a little over $5 billion.

At the same time, many have realized that as the world speeds up, we need to slow down and pay more attention to our food. In recent years, the local food and slow food movements have grown substantially. The number of USDA-registered farmers' markets doubled to 8,700 over the ten years leading up to 2016. New services such as Forager connect people to local food sources. Interest is growing in exploring the connection between our food and climate change, especially how industrial animal farms have an impact on the environment.

Time spent eating is time well spent. Besides improving digestion by eating more slowly and mindfully, we can pay attention to whether we are eating too much or too little, and what are the right foods for us. The more mindful we are of our meals, the healthier we can become.

SAME MEAL, DIFFERENT PLACE

For three weeks every summer, my parents closed their restaurant and our family took a trip to research new recipes and ideas for the business. France was a frequent destination in the early days of our travels. With reservations for lunch and dinner made months in advance, all we had to do was arrive and then eat our way across the country!

Wherever we went, my parents ordered the weirdest and most extravagant items on the menu — frogs' legs, fish heads, and calf's brains included. My sister and I had simpler tastes. At every fancy restaurant throughout France, Winnie and I ordered the same two items whether or not they were on the menu — tomato and onion salad to start, followed by roasted chicken breast.

We were visiting the most celebrated restaurants in the world at the time, presided over by legendary chefs. These giants of the culinary world took pride in the complexity and depth of their creations — sauces took days to prepare, nothing left the kitchen unless it was perfect, every detail was obsessed over. In contrast, my sister and I were asking for dishes that almost anyone could whip up.

While my parents took notes about their sophisticated culinary experiences and made plans to implement new ideas back home, my sister and I were able to truly compare chef to chef, restaurant to restaurant, based on tomato salads and roasted chicken. Looking back, these trips perhaps laid the foundation for eating as a monotask for me.

||||||||||||||||||||||||||||||||||||||||||||||||||||||||||||||||||||||||||||||||||||||||||||||||||||||||||

Why Monotasking Eating Will Help You Do Everything Better

When it comes to monotasking eating, we're going to expand our thinking in this chapter to encompass "mindful eating." Mindful eating includes deliberate thinking, learning, and listening. Each of these are good for us on their own. When combined in a subtle manner with eating, we can learn to put our monotasks together in a way that truly makes us better at everything we do.

The *thinking* I'm referring to with mindful eating involves reflection on the hard work that went into your food: growing, preparing, transporting, selling, and cooking it. If we can slow down and seek an understanding of where our food comes from, we can build stronger connections to the world.

The *learning* expands upon the thinking—we can add to our knowledge and our skills by learning more about food sources, preparation, and cooking. We may learn something new about other communities and develop more gratitude for how fortunate we are to live where we do, in these times, and make the choices we have available to us.

Mindful eating may also include *listening*, being fully present with your friends and family around the table. When we sit down with families and friends and are truly engaged, we can build stronger relationships.

The *eating* part of mindful eating is of course the primary monotask. It involves slowing down, chewing, and appreciating how food tastes and how it makes us feel. It is rare that we take the time to do this in our modern world, but our bodies can benefit when we are in closer touch with what we eat.

 ## YOUR **EATING** MONOTASK

Eat Mindfully

I hope you're hungry! We're going to do two eating monotasks — practiced at two separate meals. The first one involves eating by yourself in silence. For the second one, you will have a meal with family or friends.

Monotask 1: Eat by yourself in silence

- Set aside thirty minutes to eat your meal. I'd recommend lunch or dinner if you tend to be rushed at breakfast time.

- Do not bring any devices to the table. Think about this monotask as a *date with yourself* over a meal, without technology. If that's a scary thought, then make sure you repeat this monotask until you are comfortable with it!

- Don't worry too much about what you are going to eat except that it should be a full meal, not an energy bar or shake. Energy bars and shakes have their time and place, but for this monotask you will want to take more bites and sips than they require.

- Find a quiet place to sit and eat in silence. Ideally practice this task when you are home by yourself, but you can also find a quiet table at a restaurant, or a picnic bench outside your place of work.

- Look at your food before you eat and appreciate the colors, the aromas, and the variety. Reflect on where your food came from — how and where it was grown, prepared, cooked, and sold. Perhaps consider your ancestors and the work they put into hunting, gathering, preparing, and storing their food. Acknowledge how much easier we have it today.

- Take one bite at a time. Chew slowly and take your time between bites. Observe the tendency you may have to eat quickly and get back to something else. Take the full thirty minutes you have allotted for eating.

- Think about how a food or flavor reminds you of something in your past, a special meal, a friend's recipe, a dining experience you had on a trip. Think about how your food is passing through your system and giving you energy that allows us to work, play, think, exercise, and more.

- Observe feelings that may come up: boredom, restlessness (especially if you are used to multitasking at meals), anxiety over your to-do list, or any other emotions that surface. Make a mental note of what you feel, then let these thoughts go, and return to your meal.

- Each time thoughts unrelated to your meal rise, such as work or life issues, steer yourself back to your meal without judgment. It's normal to have our minds go in different directions — we're not used to thinking this much about our food and eating this slowly.

- At the end of your meal, silently, or out loud, express your gratitude for this meal, all the thoughts you had, and for giving yourself the gift of these thirty minutes to sit quietly and eat.

Repeat this as many times as you wish. Try to eat by yourself in silence at least once a week if you can. You can even eat with others and share this practice with them — it can be powerful to all eat in silence, slowly and deliberately.

Notice how your ability to sit in silence and take your time eating becomes more advanced over time. At first it may be hard to slow down, not check your phone, or do another task while you eat. After some practice, you should become more comfortable with this approach to eating and look forward to it. You may also evolve your diet as you get more in touch with how foods make you feel.

Monotask 2: Dinner with friends or family
- Set aside one hour for your meal.

- The meal can be home cooked, takeout, or in a restaurant. It's nice to shop for and cook your own meals, but it's not essential to start this monotask with a home-cooked meal.

- For this task, you can be somewhere quiet or loud, as part of the work is going to involve tuning out all other distractions beyond the table.

- Do not bring any devices to the table; we'll let the real world provide the distractions, not our technology.

- Let everyone know in advance what you are doing — you can describe it as monotasking or mindful eating. Or you can just tell them that you want to try a device-free dinner, and that the main conversation topics are going to be about the food.

- Thank everyone for being there. Some families pray before meals and are used to expressing gratitude at the table. However it feels right for you, take a moment to express aloud what you are grateful for — it may be that all of you are together or that all of you are trying something new. It may be the cooking, or how beautiful the food looks or smells. Take turns going around the table: really try to listen to the others and what they are grateful for. Don't judge yourself or the others, just listen.

- Before everyone starts eating, suggest that you all take your time and try to eat more slowly than usual. Take one bite at a time, put down your utensils between bites, chew slowly.

- Don't overthink what you are doing. It may be uncomfortable at first to eat more slowly, and it may not feel natural to have the conversations you will have in this monotask. Often, when we eat with the same friends or family all the time, we either don't talk much or tend to talk about the same topics — work, school, extended family, and so on. It takes a little more effort to push the conversation in new directions, but it's worth it.

- Try prompting the others to think and talk about where their food came from. Does anyone know where it was grown? How it made its way to the market? If you are at a restaurant, see if your waiter has any interesting stories about how the restaurant was started, or where their ingredients come from. Maybe the owner or chef will come over and talk with you and tell you stories.

- Tell some food stories of your own. What you loved eating growing up, which of your parents' recipes was your favorite, trips where you had a particularly delicious or adventurous meal. Ask the others about their favorite foods and encourage them to tell their food stories.

- If distractions do come up — a loud noise, a person interrupting, an interesting sight — do some or all of you lose your focus on the meal? Is it hard to bring everyone's attention back? What types of distractions can get in the way of mindful eating besides devices?

- Above all, try to be fully present at the table.

- At the end of the meal, express your gratitude to everyone again, for coming together, eating slowly, and trying something new.

Your Mantra: "Food Is Life"

It's hard to say a mantra when your mouth is full, so this one we will do silently!

Food is life can be interpreted on a few levels. Food is life itself—it has an origin, it grew, and was harvested for our consumption. Food then provides us with the fuel we need to live. Food also provides us with variety that keeps life interesting and opportunities for us to come together around the table.

The Urge to Multitask

One of my coworkers with two teenagers has a rule at home: "No Phones with Food." I like the simplicity and clarity of that. With two kids of my own, I know how hard it can be to implement a rule like this once your family has gotten into the habit of bringing phones to the table. The sooner you put this type of rule in place, and the more consistent you are about upholding it, the easier it will be to maintain in the long run.

If your family has gotten used to having devices at the table, it can be difficult to break the cycle. You could start with one night a week without devices or have a no-device rule when going out to dinner or when dining in a certain place in your house (the backyard, for example). Find a starting point that works for you and use it as an opportunity to reset the relationship between meals and devices. When smartphones and tablets first came on the scene, I don't think any of us realized how challenging they would be to keep away from the table years later.

It might take bribes or rewards to offset the power of devices and old habits. Research on establishing new habits indicates that it takes more than two months for it to become automatic. But it can take longer depending on the person and the change. Don't give up on the new habits you want to establish too quickly.

Phones and devices are not the only things that distract us from eating, of course. Going out to dinner can involve a lot of sensory overload: music, screens, open kitchens, large windows, entertaining waiters, and various displays—all these make it difficult to stay focused on your food and your table. If you tend to get distracted in environments like these, avoid them. There are plenty of quiet restaurants with a much more peaceful atmosphere—or you can have a pleasant dining experience at home.

The Reinforcements

By practicing mindful eating, we will become more aware of our food and how it makes us feel. One great reinforcement of this practice will be feeling better. Heavy, processed, or fried foods tend to make us lethargic, either immediately after eating or a few hours later. Heavy foods generally include lots of carbohydrates, starches, fats, and sugar—such as big plates of pasta, large portions of red meat, or just about anything fried.

Mindful eating may also help you get better sleep, lose weight, see improvements in your skin, or experience less stress around food and its impact on your body. All of these are good—be open to the chance that mindful eating will help your body and mind.

Growing, catching, and/or gathering your own food is also a great reinforcement. The more connection and work we put into our food, the more we appreciate it. If you can have a garden in your backyard or get space at a community garden, plant some herbs, vegetables, and whatever else appeals to you. If you're not an experienced gardener, enjoy learning about it and have fun. Don't worry too much if your tomato crop is small; you'll likely appreciate eating *any* tomato more after growing some on your own.

Visit farms and orchards. This is especially fun with children and great for them to learn where their food comes from. Pick blueberries and apples or take home some fresh meats.

Try new flavors and new foods. Go outside your comfort zone and you might discover something you love. Try shopping at a new market to increase your chance of encountering something novel. There are infinite foods to try, including from cuisines around the world.

Cook more often! If you don't know how, look up recipes online, watch videos, or take a class. Watching cooking shows can be fun and inspiring.

The Task in Your Past

We may not have practiced mindful eating in our past, but we all have eaten a lot of meals in our lifetimes. Each of us probably has a sizeable memory bank to connect to.

Do you recall roasting marshmallows as a kid? Getting the marshmallow perfectly browned and crispy? Sitting around the fire with your friends, tired from a day in the sun, carefree, and having fun?

Or can you still smell your grandmother's fresh baked pies?

How about eating corn on the cob from a local farm? Or strawberries from your family's garden?

Did you ever go down to the dock and buy shrimp or fish?

How about a favorite deli? Or bakery? I loved cinnamon raisin bagels with cream cheese from the bagel shop on Second Avenue when I was growing up in New York.

Do you recall waking up to the smell of sizzling bacon in your home? Or how much of a treat it was to go out for breakfast on a weekend and gobble up eggs, hash browns, and pancakes?

Maybe you remember the first time you had *really* good pizza. Or some of the times you ate microwaved ramen in college. Or when your roommate's parents visited and took you out to dinner somewhere fancy.

Food is seared into our brains, so to speak. Imagine the memories we can create in the decades to come if we bring more awareness to eating.

Dedicated Eaters

Around the world, food brings people together. Whether they are sitting at a table at home, at a restaurant, around a fire, in the backyard, on the front porch, a bar counter, a picnic bench, or on a beach, eating is a shared human experience. We all do it, but we also do it differently, and that makes it even more interesting to travel or sample different cuisines and traditions from where you are.

Anthony Bourdain was perhaps the world's most famous eater, traveling the world, connecting with people and cultures through food. He asked in his breakthrough book, *Kitchen Confidential*, "Do we really want to travel in hermetically sealed popemobiles through the rural provinces of France, Mexico and the Far East, eating only in Hard Rock Cafes and McDonald's? Or do we want to eat without fear, tearing into the local stew, the humble taqueria's mystery meat, the sincerely offered gift of a lightly grilled fish head?" It was a joy to watch Bourdain explore the world in his TV series *Parts Unknown* and bring a unique and new type of attention to food, politics, religion, and other dining table conversation.

Jean Anthelme Brillat-Savarin wrote what is considered to be the first book on gastronomy in 1825 — *The Physiology of Taste*. Brillat-Savarin defined the subject as follows: "Gastronomy is the reasoned comprehension of everything connected with the nourishment of man. Its aim is to obtain the preservation of man by means of the best possible nourishment. It attains this object by giving guidance, according to certain principles, to all who seek, provide or prepare substances which may be turned into food." I'm amazed that it took so long for one person to bring attention to the intersection of humans and their food as a means to cultivate their well-being. The book is not a cookbook, although it does include some recipes—it is more of a work of philosophy and a meditation on food in our lives.

Many modern-day chefs, restaurateurs, food activists, slow food movement proponents, and mindful eating thought leaders are all guiding the way into a new future for how we think about food and its role in our lives. It's nice to see all the attention being given to local food, sustainable agriculture, and eating habits that are good for the planet. Hopefully the future will involve more mindful eating for all.

FOOD ON THE SCREEN

I love movies about food, perhaps because of growing up in the restaurant business, or maybe simply because they are pleasing to multiple senses. Some of my favorites include *Tampopo, Babette's Feast, Big Night, Like Water for Chocolate,* and *Eat Drink Man Woman.* Other classics of the genre include *Soul Food, Chef,* and *Chocolat.*

While the films have very different plots, and several have international origins, one theme that unites them all is the power of an amazing meal. Films about food often show how cooking and eating play a central role in our lives, our family dynamics, and our love stories.

Even a movie like Pixar's *Ratatouille* ranks among the top food movies of all time. While the film is a hilarious comedy about a rat secretly trying to impress a Parisian kitchen with his culinary talent, the movie is also an homage to the hard work, passion, and flair that goes into cooking.

One of the finest examples of a food film that is truly a meditation on food is *Jiro Dreams of Sushi*. The documentary follows Jiro Ono, considered the world's finest sushi chef, who operates a ten-seat restaurant in Tokyo. The film is all about attention to detail and Jiro's mastery of his craft. I like to think of all the focus Jiro brings to every aspect of his restaurant as one of the ultimate expressions of monotasking.

How You'll Know You're Good at It

You'll know you are good at monotasking eating when:

- You chew slowly, appreciating each bite, and slow down at mealtime.
- You are comfortable eating in silence, without conversation or devices in hand.
- You develop a greater awareness of your body's nutritional needs, and the foods that feel right. You will know when you are full and not overeat. You will know when you are hungry and take care of yourself and your body's needs.

What if...

...you struggle with eating healthily? Developing a healthy relationship with food is very important and it is never too late to work on this. Try resetting by going off social media, magazines, and websites that bombard you with information about what to eat and what not to eat. Try mindful eating for at least thirty days and observe how different foods really make you feel.

...you are on a strict diet? Pay attention to what works for you. By practicing mindful eating and monotasking your meals, you will become more knowledgeable about your food, how it makes you feel, and how it affects your body. This can provide you with helpful information for conversations with your nutritionist or doctor and ultimately assist you in achieving the results you are aiming for.

...you are on a tight budget or live in a food desert? Healthy food can be expensive and hard to find in some places. Consider shopping online for the best prices on healthy items delivered to your doorstep using a company such as Thrive Market. Get creative with what you have left in your refrigerator or cabinets so you can stretch out the money you have already spent. Supercook is an app that tells you what you can make with ingredients you have.

...you don't have time to eat? If you have so much work to do that you cannot take time away, by all means have a working lunch or a school discussion group over takeout dinner. Even if you are eating at your desk, try to eat more mindfully and slowly. Don't try to monotask every meal right away, start with a frequency that will lead to success—for some people, one meal a week is a great starting point, for others it may be one meal a day.

...you feel guilty about eating while others do not have enough food? Consider volunteering or bringing a meal to the elderly or homeless. Make a donation to a food bank. Support sustainable agriculture and look for opportunities to improve food equity.

Overall, be positive about cultivating a new relationship with food no matter what other people have told you or how hard you have been on yourself in the past. See monotasking.tips for more ideas.

Go Eat!

Go grab a snack or have your next meal.

Eat it slowly and wait at least until you are done eating to move on to the next chapter.

TASK 6: GETTING THERE

've never been a big fan of commutes and I've always tried to live close to where I work. Perhaps I got that from my parents, as we lived above their restaurant for years. All they had to do was walk down the stairs to get to their office.

Recently, when I moved into a new house about twenty minutes from my office and my kids' schools, it was the longest commute I had experienced, although I know it's not a long commute by typical standards. When we first moved in, my internet connection was not yet set up at home so I couldn't get much work done there. And I couldn't get reliable cell phone service on my drives.

I was frustrated by my lack of productivity everywhere. Calls would drop every few minutes on the road. I started to question why I moved so far away. Then on the third day of commuting to my office, I finally gave up on trying to "do" anything on the drive.

I decided to just drive. I didn't even turn the radio on. I drove in silence, which can be hard to do if you're used to playing music, listening to the news, or making phone calls.

I varied my route every day for a while to keep things interesting. Some of the routes were more efficient than others, but each one allowed me to see something different. Horses in a field, farm stands, sunlight reflecting off a barn, abandoned cars, kids playing.

I rolled the windows down and tried to see everything as if it was the first time.

I gradually added music back in the car. I finally set up internet service at home. I switched cell phone carriers so I could make calls on the drive.

It takes a little more effort for me to monotask on my commute now that I have options, but I always try to choose monotasking whenever possible. As I have said several times before, just because technology makes it possible to multitask does not mean that we should. The dangers of multitasking while driving are too great; whatever else I need to do can wait.

This chapter is all about bringing greater attention to the task of "getting there" in order to arrive safely and happily.

The Facts About Getting There

Historically, people have been willing to accept a thirty-minute commute to get to work, something known as Marchetti's constant. As new modes of transportation have been introduced, cities have spread out, and commutes have gotten longer. As personal technology and connectivity have evolved, what we do during those thirty or more minutes each way to work has changed significantly.

Some people use their commutes to catch up on work, others to browse social media, some spend the time shopping online or watching shows. These activities all fill the time, and maybe they accomplish tasks that we don't have time for during other parts of the day. However, a 2017 study found that people with longer commutes are more likely to be depressed, have financial concerns, experience work stress, be overweight, and get less than seven hours of sleep per night. While we may be more productive and entertained on our commutes than ever before thanks to technology and connectivity, it does not counter the fact that spending more time getting to work does not, apparently, make us happy.

With respect to driving, operating a vehicle weighing several thousand pounds at high speeds has always had an element of risk. As cell phones and smartphones have proliferated, distracted driving has become more common. A 2020 survey by the insurance comparison site The Zebra found that 37.1 percent of respondents agreed that mobile phone distractions impair one's ability to drive safely—yet 28.6 percent admitted that they texted while driving.

The consequences of distracted driving are significant. In 2018, according to the National Highway Traffic Safety Administration, an estimated 400,000 people were injured due to distracted driving, with 2,841 lives lost.

While there are laws and educational initiatives in place to curb distracted driving, some believe that our greatest hope to address the problem is a future where self-driving cars save us from ourselves. In *21 Lessons for the 21st Century*, Yuval Noah Harari estimates that if all drivers were replaced by computers, road deaths and injuries would be reduced by around 90 percent. Until that future arrives, we need to pay more attention on the roads.

TIME FOR A UVAC!

During my college days in New Hampshire, occasionally I would head out for a drive with friends on what we called a UVAC, an Upper Valley Appreciation Cruise — the area surrounding Dartmouth College was referred to as the Upper Valley.

These cruises were part cure for burnout from studying but they also served as a local economic stimulus. Our cruises rarely had a destination. We didn't consult the internet (it wouldn't have been that helpful back then) and we didn't own any guidebooks. There was some advice from older students — "Get the Reuben at the Fairlee Diner!" — but most of the time, we were guided only by our intuition.

If a country road looked interesting, we took it. If a roadside stop was tempting, we pulled over. Often, we'd discover a diner and load up on greasy food or eat breakfast for dinner. Or we'd come across a cheese maker with delicious cheddar, or a maple syrup farm down a dirt lane.

The drives took us across covered bridges, along winding rivers, and through forests. As a city kid who had grown up taking buses and subways nearly my whole life, these cruises were magical. My eyes were wide open the whole time.

The only conversations were between friends in the car. The soundtrack was provided by a mix tape that one of us had spent hours making. Sometimes the main excuse for taking a UVAC was to premiere a new mix!

Why Monotasking Getting There Will Help You Do Everything Better

The primary goal of monotasking getting there is to arrive safely, pure and simple. It's highly likely that the greatest risk in the average person's day is concentrated around the times that they are in transit from one place to another. Becoming more focused while in proximity to heavy machinery traveling at high speed is good for us, and all those we pass by en route.

The second goal of monotasking the act of getting there is to be more present on our journeys, to see and appreciate many of the finer details in life. Whether it is traveling to a new country or repeating your usual commute, there is always something new to see, smell, or hear. Depending on your mode of transportation, you will have different capacities to take in this information without multitasking or losing focus.

For example, if you are riding a high-speed train you will get somewhere quickly but the journey may be a blur. In contrast, when traveling by rickshaw or on the back of a moped, you may see so much that you can't process it all. Seeing different perspectives, new things, and finer detail are all great skills that will help you throughout your life. Our travel experiences can really benefit our understanding of other cultures, help us develop empathy, and allow us to practice our powers of observation. The more we pay attention while we travel, the more stories we will also have to tell back home!

Another benefit of focusing on getting there and *not* multitasking on the way is that we can do everything better on its own once we arrive. I understand the desire to be productive at all times, but our work quality will always improve if we give it our full attention. When you are traveling, simply ask yourself if you are able to give your work your full focus. If you are the one driving, I'll answer that question for you with an emphatic "no" — your attention is needed at the steering wheel.

Perhaps counterintuitively, monotasking getting there can also help improve our social relationships. We *think* we should respond to messages from friends and family as quickly as possible — but strong friendships are generally based on qualities deeper than response time. Overall responsiveness is important, but good friends should be patient, appreciate your full attention when you have it to give, and value your safety and that of others around you.

YOUR GETTING THERE MONOTASK

Focus on the Journey

In Jenny Odell's *How to Do Nothing: Resisting the Attention Economy,* she recounts a story of how she and a friend explored a creek that connected their lives in northern California. She writes, "Nothing is so simultaneously familiar and alien as that which has been present all along." Odell goes on to describe the details of what they encounter along the creek in Cupertino and points out that when we notice something we may have previously taken for granted, it "begins to reveal its significance."

We will practice two monotasks around the activity of getting there. The first is to bring awareness to when we become bored on a journey, which is often when the temptation to multitask begins. The second is to cultivate a sense of wonder while on a journey, much like Odell's story, by paying attention and letting details reveal themselves to us.

Monotask 1: Recognize when you're bored

- Identify an upcoming journey that will be longer than twenty minutes during which you will be able to practice this monotask. It can be your commute or a leisure trip by car, bus, train, boat, plane, or other mode of transportation.

- For the first few times you practice this monotask, you should be a passenger, not the driver. This is so that you can give your full focus to the monotask (referring to this chapter as necessary). Once you have experience with the steps, then you can and should also practice it while driving.

- Once on the trip, try to do nothing except experience yourself being transported from one place to another.

- Turn off the radio and do not wear headphones.

- Don't do any work; just sit and look out the window. Are you able to sit still and watch the world go by?

- See if you can identify when you become bored.

- What happens when boredom sinks in? Do you reach for your phone? What other reactions do you have?

- If your notifications are turned on, can you resist the temptation to look at them or browse your phone to fill the time? If you aren't able to ignore your phone, I recommend turning it off. Know yourself and what you are capable of. Be aware of what remains difficult for you when monotasking and then you can adapt your approach to minimize distractions.

- Are you tempted to turn on music or the news?

- Boredom can be a healthy feeling to experience. We have all gotten used to being able to move on from boredom quickly, often via our smartphones. Observe how boredom makes you feel and what your reaction to it is — especially if it seems like a multitasking temptation.

Monotask 2: Cultivate a sense of wonder

- For this task, again choose a journey longer than twenty minutes, and where you are the passenger. (As with Monotask 1 above, you should also return to this task later as a driver.)

- Put your phone out of view and set it to Do Not Disturb.

- Don't do any work or handle any devices while you are getting there.

- Travel without the radio or other sound on. *Listen* to the inside and outside your mode of transportation — the noise of your vehicle, the soundtrack of the city, conversations you overhear, the wind, the silence.

- Enjoy the view. Observe what you *see* in front of you, out the side windows, and inside your mode of transportation. Look at the colors, the textures, and the variety.

- If you are traveling at high speed, try to slow things down with your eyes and pick out a detail as it whirs by — a sign, an animal, or a building.

- Then make your vision wider and try to capture the overall feeling of the world as it moves by (only with your eyes and your brain, not an actual photograph). Is it like an abstract expressionist painting? A high-resolution image? A color, a mood, something else?

- What is the weather? What does it look, feel, and smell like? Have you experienced this weather before? Does it bring back a memory?

- Feel the motor. What does it sound like? Is your seat solid or loose — what happens when you go around turns versus accelerate on a straightaway? Think about those who invented the mode of transportation you are in, and those who manufactured your specific vehicle. How many people contributed to getting it to the point where *you* could get inside and go places?

- Express gratitude (either silently or out loud) to the people whose job it is to get you to where you are going safely. This may include the driver, those who made and maintain the vehicle, the roads, tracks, airports, and other infrastructure.

- When you arrive, acknowledge that you have completed your getting there monotask and you are moving on to something else. Thank yourself for paying attention on the journey.

Your Mantra: "Enjoy the Journey"

Our mantra for this monotask is *Enjoy the journey.*

No matter whether you've made a trip one thousand times, or it's the first time, enjoy the journey. Repeat the mantra as you fly, drive, ride the train, or cruise on the water.

We can find joy in every aspect of life when we stay present.

The Urge to Multitask

On his late-night show, James Corden has a recurring segment called Carpool Karaoke in which he takes a drive with a famous passenger and they sing songs and have a fun conversation. I should relax and enjoy the segments with artists including Paul McCartney and Adele, but I confess they always tend to stress me out—I worry about James and his guests getting into a distracted driving accident! I was relieved to find out that some of the segments are filmed with the car being towed so that James can focus on singing and charming his guests, not on driving...phew!

For the rest of us who are *not* being towed to our destinations, getting there distractions might resemble these:

A call will come in.

A text will arrive.

Your phone will notify you of something.

The song on the radio may be terrible, or the news boring or upsetting.

A story on the radio, an audiobook, or podcast may be extremely engaging and pull you completely into it.

Something may grab your attention out the window, such as an accident.

Your kids, dog, or something inside the car might distract you.

The temperature may be uncomfortable.

You may miss a turn or your stop.

Someone next to you may be distracting or annoying.

A thought will pop into your head, and you may go deeply into thinking about something else.

It's helpful to expect distractions to happen and be prepared for what you will do when they occur. I learned to drive in New York City and I remember my father telling me, "Always expect someone to do the craziest thing imaginable right in front of you. What will you do if the taxi in the left lane suddenly swings across four lanes of traffic to pick up a passenger on the right side of the road?" A situation like that can call really upon your monotasking skills in a nanosecond! Most of the distractions and multitasking temptations you face while getting there will not be this intense.

In most cases, you should simply acknowledge distractions as they arise and let them go, then return to focusing on getting there safely. If you need to deal with an interruption, pull over if you are the driver, then give the other task your attention. For ideas that pop into your head, if you can do so safely, record a quick voice memo to your phone with your thoughts, then replay it when you arrive.

The Reinforcements

If you are the driver, it is important to do everything possible to maintain your focus on the road. Apple has a "Do Not Disturb While Driving" setting that can automatically detect when you are driving, then block all notifications, and many Android phones have a similar function. It also auto-sends a response to a person who texts letting them know you are driving. They then have the option to mark their message "Urgent," in which case it will come through and you can then pull over to respond. As technology evolves quickly, see monotasking.tips for the latest recommendations on apps and settings that will reinforce your ability to get there safely.

Other strategies include giving your phone to a passenger, turning your phone off, or placing it somewhere you cannot see or hear it. At the very least, you should go hands-free — use Bluetooth, Apple CarPlay, or another system for making and receiving phone calls. Remember also that just because your hands are free from your phone does not mean that your attention is not dangerously diverted by other cognitive tasks. Be aware of where your attention is while driving.

Make an agreement with passengers as well as friends and

family you frequently communicate with about how responsive you will be en route, whether on a short drive or a long vacation. Consider sending a text before you leave saying that you will be driving and unable to respond until a certain time, then do not look at your phone until you get there.

When you are driving, set a good example for your passengers and your children by not using your phone. Ask for assistance with the radio and other controls so you can keep your eyes on the road. Make specific agreements about everyone's multitasking and technology usage before you depart, then hold each other accountable. An agreement might be that no one can use their phone on a trip so that *all* of you can look out the window and appreciate the journey. Or it might be that one person is in charge of your phone and responding to important messages while you drive.

The Task in Your Past

Did you love trains, planes, construction vehicles, and/or automobiles as a kid? A lot of children love watching machines move and playing with toy versions of them. There is a sense of wonder and awe when a child looks up at a helicopter in the sky, or at a passing train.

Whether or not you were into machines that moved as a kid, we can all connect with a child's appreciation for how cool transportation technology is. Machines get us to work, back home, and off to faraway places, but they are also pretty fascinating destinations in themselves for our mind.

Did you enjoy looking out the window of a moving vehicle when you were younger? Marveling at everything that you saw and feeling the air rushing by? Try to connect with the sense of wonder that you experienced earlier in your life—both when you travel and on your routine excursions. The world is vast and complex; our capacity to experience it through our senses and our cognitive capabilities, and our ability to get just about anywhere we want to go on the planet is amazing.

There was a time when we didn't have as much on our minds as we do now. Back then we were just excited to go places. Much of the thinking we processed en route was simply how excited we were to get there. Tap into the simplicity of past journeys, the joy of getting there, and the anticipation of where you were going.

Dedicated Travelers

There is a great tradition of travel writing, from which we can learn many things about paying attention to details while we are on the move.

One of the earliest surviving works of the genre is *The Travels of Marco Polo*. Polo was a thirteenth-century Venetian merchant who traveled the Silk Road in Asia. He was also an amazing observer of details on his journeys through the Mongol Empire and China. He recounted, "I did not tell half of what I saw, for I knew I would not be believed." The idea that it is possible for one to experience so much on a journey that the story cannot possibly be told in full is remarkable in itself. We often condense our stories after a trip to the greatest hits, only we know what we experienced and how expansive it was.

Mark Twain wrote in *The Innocents Abroad*, "Travel is fatal to prejudice, bigotry, and narrow-mindedness, and many of our people need it sorely on these accounts. Broad, wholesome, charitable views of men and things cannot be acquired by vegetating in one little corner of the earth all one's lifetime." The idea that we can open our minds and improve our ability to relate to other people through traveling is quite powerful and a great incentive for all of us to hit the road.

In 1996, *Under the Tuscan Sun* by Frances Mayes was published and subsequently inspired many others to travel, discover their true selves far from home, and tell their stories to the world. In the memoir, the author recounts her experience living in Italy, restoring an old villa, eating local delicacies, and interacting with memorable personalities. She writes, "Life offers you a thousand chances...all you have to do is take one."

Robert Frost wrote about a more simplified choice:

Two roads diverged in a wood, and I—
I took the one less traveled by,
And that has made all the difference.

Whether you have the option of two roads or a thousand chances, keep moving, stay focused, and observe the details of life with your full attention.

GETTING THERE WITH SOME DIFFICULTY

Every year, my son and I go on a winter trip to a cabin in the Colorado wilderness along with a few other families. The cabins we reserve are not accessible by road. The first few times we went on these trips, we all snowshoed in together. This past year, I decided to travel on backcountry skis.

While I had used my skis to get some fun powder runs in, I had not yet attempted anything as far (six miles), as high (11,400 feet), or as cold (zero degrees Fahrenheit) as this trip entailed. Six miles may not sound like a lot for a hike, but when it's up at high altitude, involves steep trails, and you're towing a heavy sled filled with food and gear, the effort required to get there was herculean.

Even though I was in decent cardiovascular shape, I found myself struggling with the elevation and experienced a variety of equipment failures and physical pains on the way up. I paused to stretch my back and hips, stopped to repair my broken waist belt, and took frequent breaks just to catch my breath.

I also had a near constant dialogue in my head about how hard the trek was, why did I pack so much stuff, and why didn't I just snowshoe like everyone else? About two-thirds of the way up the mountain, I decided to reset my mind and my focus. I shifted my attention to be that of a passenger on the journey, and not the driver/engine that I actually was.

From that point forward, I observed everything we passed as if I was seeing it for the first time—snow-covered trees, remnants of old mining shacks in the forest, mountains and alpine lakes in the distance. I turned the physical activity (and the pain it was causing) into a background task so that I could get to where we were going.

After six and a half hours, I finally arrived at the cabin and could relax. We took turns tending the wood-burning stove, cooking meals, sledding, and playing games. The hard effort was worth it in the end.

How You'll Know You're Good at It

You'll know you are good at your getting there monotask when:

- You travel in a manner that is consistently safe for you and others on your journey.
- You experience joy in your travels and on your commute, regardless of whether you are the driver or the passenger.
- You realize that much of your stress has been left behind.

- You are more able to pay attention to the journey, notice new details, and not be distracted by your devices, your work, or other things on your mind.
- You aren't bored or impatient to get there, or at least you are able to recognize when you become bored and work through the feelings.
- You are patient about waiting until you arrive to accomplish your other tasks. You are able to resist the temptation to multitask while in transit.
- You look forward to future trips.

What if...

...you have a career where you have to work in your car? If it can't be avoided, set up your technology in order to minimize the distractions of looking up phone numbers and other information. These tasks should be voice activated and allow you to keep your hands on the wheel.

...you are in the middle of a big breakup/fight/deal? Don't drive when experiencing strong emotions, as they can contribute to aggressive or distracted driving. At the very least, pull over and park so that you can focus on communicating and not put anyone else at risk.

...you live really far from work or repeat a monotonous journey often? If you are the one doing the driving, approach the trips with curiosity. Practice monotasking your journey and experimenting with different routes. Try carpooling or taking public transportation so that your attention can be freed up to look out the window, listen to an audiobook, podcast, or learn something new.

...you really want to travel but don't have the resources? Some of the greatest adventures have been executed on the smallest of budgets. Sometimes spending less can help you enjoy the journey even more. Take a staycation, swap houses with a friend, drive instead of flying, or go camping (even in the backyard is fun!).

...there's no way for you to get out of town? In addition to the close-to-home ideas mentioned above, you can also experience "armchair travel" through reading—travelogues, novels, and photo-illustrated books about other lands. Watch a documentary or a foreign film, visit a museum in real life or virtually. Find a recipe for an exotic dish and give it a try or download an app to learn a foreign language. These things won't replace the experience of actually traveling to a different place, but they can help us get by and still absorb many of the lessons of monotasking travel.

Get There!

Go for a drive, hop on a bus, ride a bike, paddle a canoe, or fly somewhere. Take in the sights, the sounds, and the smells on the journey. But most of all, make sure you get there safely.

TASK 7: LEARNING

My ninth grade French teacher thought I was the worst language student she had ever had in her class. I had been studying French for four years at that point and I thought I was pretty good at it. Madame B. felt very differently.

Madame B. didn't just give me bad grades, she seemed intent on making clear to me, the other students in the class, and my parents that I was incapable of learning French or any language. Every few minutes in her classroom, I was in trouble for one thing or another—using improper grammar, being on the wrong page of the textbook, or playing the wrong part of a recording in the language lab. On homework assignments and tests, I came to expect lots of red ink and low scores.

At the end of the year, I decided to drop French altogether and enroll in Spanish for the first time. When I started tenth grade, my Spanish teacher, Señora M., thought I was a language genius! I got all A's and every time Señora M. called on me, I had the right answers. She even asked me to help the other students who were struggling with their Spanish. Señora M. referred to me as a "gifted language student."

So which one was it? Was I a terrible student or was I good at learning languages? Was I just bad at French and good at Spanish?

Did I become a better learner over a few months as I matured from age fourteen to fifteen?

I thought about these questions for years. Being told I was a bad student and could not learn something weighed on me into my adult life. When I was twenty-nine, I decided to do something about it.

I signed up for a weeklong French immersion class so I could figure out once and for all whether I was capable of learning French. It was essentially summer camp for adults and it would either be a miserable struggle or a great learning experience.

Starting on day one, my French skills came right back—monotasking French for the week was just what I needed. The program director moved me to a more advanced group on day two and I welcomed the challenge. I learned more French vocabulary and grammar that week than I probably learned in all of ninth grade.

Now I'm able to tell a different, more confident, story about myself than the one Madame B. told about me years ago. I'm glad that I took the time to turn a negative learning experience early in life into a positive one many years later.

Learning new skills is one way we can rewrite the story of our lives. Whether it is to pursue a different career, for our own intellectual curiosity, or to strengthen our ability to focus, monotasking learning can be very rewarding.

The Facts About Learning

Some people are under the mistaken impression that it's not possible to learn new things when we grow up. How many times have you heard the expression, *You can't teach an old dog new tricks*? However, a concept called neuroplasticity describes how the brain is capable of learning at all ages. Michael Merzenich, PhD, explains in his book *Soft-Wired: How the New Science of Brain Plasticity Can Change Your Life*, "If a brain is exercised properly, anyone can grow intelligence, at any age, and potentially by a lot. Or you can just let your brain idle—and watch it slowly, inexorably, go to seed like a sedentary body."

Not only is the brain capable of learning new material and new skills, but it is also good for our brains to continue learning throughout our lives—this helps prevent cognitive decline. The "Finnish Geriatric Intervention Study to Prevent Cognitive Impairment and Disability" followed a group of older individuals in a two-year study and determined that a combination of nutritional guidance, exercise, cognitive training, and social activity led to better results on neuropsychological tests than a control group.

There are some amazing examples of learning achievements by adults around the world when they put their minds to it. As John Basinger of Connecticut, a retired theater professor, approached his sixtieth birthday, he decided to challenge himself by memorizing all of John Milton's epic poem, *Paradise Lost*—more than sixty thousand words. Not only did Basinger succeed at his challenge, but he performed the piece on multiple occasions. How long did a recitation take from beginning to end? A staggering twenty-four hours!

LEARNING FROM EVERY EXPERIENCE

In 1999, I started a company called Feedback Direct. My idea was to create one website where customers could get service from thousands of companies in one place. As a consumer, I had seen how hard it was to find a company's contact information online. As an entrepreneur, I wanted to make it easier to submit complaints, compliments, and questions to any business. Our team at Feedback Direct would follow up to make sure that customers received a response.

I was young and idealistic about how the internet could change the world and what role I could play in the technology revolution. I pitched my idea to investors and was able to raise some startup capital. For the next two years, I worked nonstop to try to bring my vision into reality with the help of a team of about twelve. We built a website and developed email management software. And then we ran out of money before we had ever generated a dollar in revenue.

The business model was flawed—it turned out that businesses didn't want another company getting between them and their customers, especially when there were complaints involved. Despite the fact that Feedback Direct went out of business, I never considered it to be a failure. I learned invaluable lessons about starting a business, hiring and managing a team, communicating with investors, and much more.

I certainly learned the hard way that we should have talked to potential customers earlier than we did. It would have been smart to ask businesses what they would have been willing to pay for, and also how we could modify our systems to address their concerns. I also learned a lot about work–life balance and not pushing myself to the point of exhaustion. There is a lot to be learned when things don't work out as planned.

Why Monotasking Learning Will Help You Do Everything Better

We can learn to do anything, and we should keep our minds open throughout our lives. There is a concept in Zen Buddhism called "beginner's mind." A beginner's mind is open, willing to learn, accepts that we don't know anything, and therefore is free from any preconceptions about learning. Shunryū Suzuki writes in *Zen Mind, Beginner's Mind: Informal Talks on Zen Meditation and Practice*, "In the beginner's mind there are many possibilities, but in the expert's there are few."

Let's consider the opposite of the beginner's mind as the "know-it-all" for the sake of simplicity. Most would consider the know-it-all persona as annoying. The majority of us are somewhere in between the beginner's mind and the know-it-all on various topics. Sometimes we don't like to admit what we don't know; sometimes we feel pressure to act like an expert.

The person who is open to learning and who has more of a beginner's mind is generally much more receptive to the world and all the things there are to learn. And there is so much to learn—we only experience a small part of the world in our lifetimes!

Learning can truly help us with anything we want to know or do, and it can help us build connections with other people. We can be the student and they can be the teacher, and that bond, plus the empathy it generates, is extraordinary.

Even if you are stuck in a job you don't like, you can learn something new while there—perhaps a computer skill, how to run meetings more effectively, or an accounting procedure—that you can take with you to a new position. Or you can be receptive to learning in your personal life and achieve personal growth, perhaps through reading, taking workshops, or traveling. We should keep ourselves open to learning and monotask it.

YOUR LEARNING MONOTASK

Learn Something New

In David Epstein's book *Range: Why Generalists Triumph in a Specialized World,* he shares an important insight: "Whether chemists, physicists, or political scientists, the most successful problem solvers spend mental energy figuring out what type of problem they are facing before matching a strategy to it, rather than jumping in with memorized procedures." This is true also for learning — a lot of times we leap into a learning task without taking the time to get organized about *how* we should learn.

This first monotask below is focused on spending some time and attention getting ready to learn. The second task is about the learning itself. It does not really matter what you set out to learn in these tasks, as long as you learn something you do not already know.

Monotask 1: Make a learning plan

- Find a quiet space and set aside at least twenty minutes. Have a few sheets of paper and a pen handy.

- Put down your phone and turn off notifications.

- Choose something to learn. It could be all the prime numbers under a hundred. Or memorizing the Gettysburg Address. Or how to count to ten in Japanese or another language. For now, choose something that you think you can learn in about twenty minutes.

- Whatever you choose to learn, it should not require any tools or materials other than what you have readily available without shopping or too much digging around.

- Make a learning plan — that is what this task is all about. Make a list of all the different ways you *could* learn to do whatever you chose. Your list might include reading a book, watching a video, taking a class, just doing it, asking an expert, and so on. Don't do any of these things yet!

- Narrow down your list to the method or methods that appeal most to you and think will work best with your learning style.

- Now think through the steps that you will follow to learn what you chose to learn and write them down. Your notes should look like an instructional sheet with numbered steps in the order you plan to follow them.

- Also write down how much time you think you will need to learn this new skill. Will additional resources be required? How many times do you think you'll need to repeat the steps to learn what you set out to learn?

- Dedicate all of your attention to making this plan. That is the full task.

- Once you have a plan, you are finished with this first monotask. Take some time off before you come back to the second monotask.

Monotask 2: Learn to do something new

- Return to your learning plan a few hours later or on a different day from making it and set aside as much time as you determined in the monotask above that you would need.

- Follow the plan that you created in Monotask 1.

- Stick with it, even if you get distracted and even if you realize that you didn't get everything exactly right in your plan. The point is both to learn *how* to learn *and* to learn the new skill.

- Observe yourself, and learn from the experience. What did you realize about your ability to make a learning plan? Did you discover something about how you learn best? What would you do differently next time?

- Repeat both monotasks with other skills you want to learn.

Your Mantra: "I've Got Room in My Brain for More."

There's a popular myth that says we use only 10 percent or less of our brains, but that is not true at all. Exactly how much we use depends on what we are doing, but it is certainly more than 10 percent, and there is definitely room for us to add more to our brains.

Our learning mantra is longer than the others in this book, but I'm certain you have room in your brain for it!

When you are learning something new, say or think: *I've got room in my brain for more.* Then load up on new information and skills!

The Urge to Multitask

The internet is a great place to learn new things, but it can also be super distracting when we go in search of classes, how-tos, and videos. (We've probably all dived down internet rabbit holes we had no intention of entering!) It can be tempting to surf from one interesting video to another, or look up all the experts on a particular topic, so much so that it can be hard to get started and super easy to get sidetracked from actually learning anything.

How do we keep our learning monotask focused while being tempted by so many distractions? It can seem that multitasking distractions are tailor-made for us, as if YouTube really knows what video we are looking for while we are watching another one. The reality is that they *do* know, and they want you to multitask, at least in terms of *Watch this, then that, and watch an ad every now and then, too.*

If we are using the internet to learn, we have to accept that tech companies are really good at putting information in front of us that we *think* we want and need. We often don't know whether to be grateful or afraid that Instagram, TikTok, and Apple can ostensibly read our minds!

Before embarking on an internet-enabled learning adventure, I suggest writing down what you are looking for, like a shopping list when you go to the grocery store. Make an agreement with yourself that you are going to stay focused and stick to your goal. A sample plan might be "I'm going to spend twenty minutes practicing my Spanish" or "I'm going to find a video to learn to play a Beatles song on my guitar." Then when you get tempted to look at or do something else, refer back to your plan and steer yourself back on track. No judgment, no shame, just recognize that the deck is stacked against you (by "Big Tech" and the attention economy) and that you're doing the best you can.

You can bookmark interesting content and come back to it another day or you can use a program that limits your time online (essentially turning off internet access after a certain time frame). Visit monotasking.tips for more suggestions on tools that you can use to keep your learning monotask focused.

Distracting things can also happen offline. You might get bored if you are reading a book, listening to a lecture, or walking through a museum and your mind starts to wander. When boredom sets in for me in the offline world, I like to remind myself what a gift it is to be able to learn without the internet or a screen in this day and age. Overall, I can be much more focused and immersed when learning offline—some momentary internal boredom is better than constant external attempts to intercept my attention and divert it.

The Reinforcements

Sometimes the incentives provided by society, corporations, academia, or social media are not truly aligned with learning and self-improvement. We should be aware of this and get in touch with what reinforces our own internal learning capabilities. Seeking external rewards, doing things out of obligation, or being too focused on growing our fans and followers may not provide the long-lasting reinforcement we need.

Here are some ideas for reinforcing your learning monotask:

- Connect with how you feel when you learn something new. It's a marvel of the human body and brain that we can always learn new things. Sometimes we take it for granted when we learn something new and don't notice how it makes us feel. Be sure to pay attention to how you feel after you learn and how incredible it is to be able to expand your knowledge and skills.

- Celebrate learning. Mark the occasion, no matter how small, with a celebration. Whether it's going out for dinner, buying yourself a present, or just doing a celebratory dance, go for it.

- Tell the story! It's an accomplishment to learn something new. Go ahead and share with your friends and family— online if you want, but definitely in real life. You can brag, or be humble, make it funny or self-deprecating ("I never thought I'd be able to install my own bathroom tile..."). Be supportive when others tell you what they learned.

- Practice, practice, practice. Practicing what we have learned is one of the best ways to absorb and master a skill. You don't need to spend ten thousand hours on practice; start by giving whatever you are practicing your full attention and see what you can learn.

- Observe from a distance. Sometimes when you are super close to learning something new, you don't notice how much progress you are making. Take a video or make a recording of your progress (I know that sounds like a violation of monotasking but it's for a good reason) then watch or listen to it later in order to reflect on how much progress you are making.

- Learn from masters. Mastery of a skill is what happens when you have learned something to the point where you can essentially do it without thinking. For every skill on the planet, there is someone who has mastered it, and we can learn a lot from them. Seek out a fluent speaker, a virtuoso, a brilliant orator. They weren't born that way. They learned their way to mastery.

- Break things down into bite-size, manageable chunks. Learning a lot at once can be overwhelming and discouraging, but don't let it get to you. When I learn a new song on the guitar, I break it down into sections and learn them separately, then put them together. Break apart what you are learning and don't bite off more than you can chew!

- Don't be afraid to make mistakes. Often, we learn more from our mistakes than our successes. The more experiences we have, the more we can learn. By doing more, we will inevitably make some mistakes.

- Don't be afraid to make a fool out of yourself!

The Task in Your Past

"Did you read the instructions?" My dad would always ask me that when I was growing up and putting something together. I confess, I didn't like to read the instructions — I wanted to jump right in and start making things!

It may have been a new stereo I was setting up, or a model of the *Titanic* I was building. To me, I was still learning and doing, even if I wasn't doing it in the right order, and even if I had to redo some steps later. Now my son is the one who reminds me to read the instructions whenever we are building something!

My father and my son are both right; I should read the instructions. But sometimes I just don't want to. I want to figure things out as I go — it's not like I'm building a thermonuclear reactor, we're mostly talking about IKEA furniture here.

Don't give up on learning just because someone said something to you in the past that made you think you were not doing a task the right way or that you were not capable of learning. There are lots of ways to learn and we can figure out what works for us individually over time.

Neil Fleming created the VARK framework to help assess learning modalities, an approach that can be used in schools, groups, businesses, sports, and other teaching and learning forums. The V stands for Visual learning (through images, charts, graphs, illustrations, etc.), A for Aural (by hearing, repetition, reading out loud, videos, etc.), R for Read/Write (reading, taking notes, writing summaries, essays, etc.), and K for Kinesthetic (by doing, hands-on activities, demonstrations, and movement). Thinking of these different approaches to learning are helpful for monotasking learning (and teaching!). If one way doesn't work for you, try another—don't give up.

Talented Learners

The media tends to glamorize people with one big idea, one big hit, one big breakthrough—the blockbuster movie, the billion-dollar startup, the medical innovation. Usually these sensational stories represent the tip of the iceberg in terms of the learning that went on behind the scenes to get to that one big thing. There are a lot more stories of learning that don't make headlines, yet they still make the world go around.

We should draw inspiration from people who have committed to lifelong learning—they are everywhere! We should celebrate the doctors who learn new surgical techniques, the accountants who absorb the latest tax codes, and the pilots who stay current on their safety training. Travelers who want to experience a culture more directly might learn a new language before departing. Those who realize something is missing in the world learn how to make it happen—maybe they land a deal on *Shark Tank* or maybe they just have a cool contraption in their garage.

LIFELONG LEARNING

I love learning new things and I also enjoy discovering new ways to learn. For me, it's not about being the best at any one particular skill; I primarily want to make life interesting and fun. Some of the skills and approaches to learning that I have experimented with have included:

Playing piano. I started taking piano lessons when I was seven years old, then pretty much stopped playing when I was twelve. Recently I decided to relearn piano and set out to explore a variety of learning methods until I found one that worked for me. I have since learned to play a number of songs by watching videos from YouTube creators, including PHianonize.

Playing guitar. Guitar followed piano, but when I got to college, I didn't think I was good enough to play in a band, so I gave it up for a few decades. I started taking lessons again when my daughter wanted to learn guitar. It was a great opportunity for the two of us to go to music lessons and practice together.

Dog training. I had not had a dog in my adult life until adopting the sweetest puppy in the world, Maple. To learn how to train her properly, I watched YouTube videos (mostly from Zak George) and read several books. I don't remember if we really trained the dogs in our family when I was growing up, but whatever we did, it was very different from my approach with Maple. She is a great dog and I'm proud of everything that both she and I learned in the process!

How to be a better human! I try lots of new things all the time. I'm constantly absorbing bits of wisdom here and there from books, workshops, classes, podcasts, conversations, and travel. I put them to use in my life, see what's effective and resonates with me, then seek out new ideas and make more adjustments. I hope I never get tired of learning, or trying new approaches to learning; there is so much to explore.

How You'll Know You're Good at It

One goal of learning may be to develop your own mastery of a skill or subject. "In the end, mastery involves discovering the most resonant information and integrating it so deeply and fully it disappears and allows us to fly free," explains Josh Waitzkin in *The Art of Learning: An Inner Journey to Optimal Performance*. You'll know you are good at learning when:

- You look forward to taking on more learning challenges.
- You appreciate how hard it is to learn something and how hard others have worked to develop their skills. As we learn something, we tend to develop a greater respect for people and experts who are really good at it.
- You want to share what you have learned with others, possibly teaching them how to do it as well.

What if...

...you have a learning disability? My friend Emily works with students who have learning disabilities, including dyslexia and ADHD, and she shared some great advice with me. If you have a learning disability, first recognize that you are intelligent and that you learn differently from others. Chances are that you were not properly

diagnosed in school or given the opportunity to learn in a manner that worked for you. Be patient and don't measure yourself by what others are doing or how long it takes you to read or learn. Find a subject that is interesting to you, possibly one that you have some experience with already—this will make you much more motivated to learn and your confidence will build much more quickly as you add to your knowledge.

...*you think you're not a good student or incapable of learning?* Perhaps you were told this by a teacher, administrator, or manager and this story has stayed with you for some time. Consider that the opposite might be true, that you are an excellent student and highly capable of learning, but you just need to do it a little differently from the mainstream traditional method of sitting in class, reading books, and so on. Try learning by experience (going out and doing it), learning visually (by watching videos), or listening (podcasts, audiobooks, radio, etc.).

...*you think you're too old to learn anything new?* We're always capable of learning. Find something you are interested in learning and give monotasking it a try. Never give up!

...*you think your brain is full?* There's plenty of room in your brain. When you add knowledge and skills to it, you don't have to clear out other material to make room; it doesn't work that way. If anything, your other knowledge and skills will be improved by using your brain more to do new things.

...*you just don't have time?* Try reframing your definition of learning. It's not something that always requires sitting in a class or taking a lesson. Instead, envision learning as something that can happen anywhere, anytime, and only takes a few minutes. Maybe you try learning one word a day in a foreign language, learning part of a song or dance over several days, or tackling a home project a little at a time.

Go Learn!

Go learn something new and have fun with it! There are so many choices—try not to get overwhelmed, and don't worry about mastering anything. Find what appeals to you and see where it leads you in life.

TASK 8: TEACHING

Teaching can help us focus in many ways. When we bring our attention to one thing that we are teaching, we approach it differently than when we are rushing around in the rest of our lives. We slow down. We break down the information into segments and steps. We think about whether our audience is paying attention and learning.

In the same way that we are constantly learning throughout our lives, we also have daily opportunities to teach others. Everyone in life is a teacher, in one way or another.

It may be subtle — showing by example how to react or not react in a difficult situation. Or it may be more obvious — teaching a friend how to make your favorite recipe, or your children how to ride a bike.

In my day-to-day life, I'm constantly learning and teaching all the time. I've never been a paid teacher, and I've only been in front of a classroom as an adult a handful of times as a guest speaker. However, I'm always teaching my kids new things, and they teach me as well. I frequently coach my team at the office on how to best serve our customers, and when they discover a new way to do things, they teach me. I mentor those who seek me out for advice about starting a business and other topics, and I seek out others who have the experience and expertise to mentor me. These are all forms of teaching and learning.

It may not be something you think about often, but you have skills and knowledge that you can pass on to others. And like all the other tasks in this book, it's best done with focus. When you teach, bringing all of your attention to teaching as a monotask will help you be the best teacher, develop greater confidence and mastery of your own skills and knowledge, and connect with your "student(s)" to help them learn.

Not only does teaching make us better at what we know and do, it builds connections to others, and it helps us organize our brain in ways that we can apply to other areas of life.

Monotasking teaching is about becoming better at everything you do, and helping others do the same.

The world is a complex place. There is a lot to learn and there is a need for really good teachers—not just in our schools, but in everyday life. If we can all become better teachers, transmitting our knowledge of small things (like how to set the clock on the microwave) and large issues (how to address climate change) to others, we can improve the world we live in.

The Facts About Teaching

According to the World Bank, there are more than ninety million teachers in the world. Those are the people who get paid to teach at all levels of education. But all of us at one point or another teach others what we know. We probably don't get paid for it, and we may not even be thanked for it, but it is innately human to convey knowledge to others.

During the pandemic, many parents discovered just how hard it is to take on school teaching responsibilities for children at home. It can be challenging enough to teach kids manners and how to do chores: add in math and history lessons, and we're quickly overwhelmed, exhausted, and wishing for things to return to normal.

Most working parents did not have the luxury to monotask the teaching of their children during school closures, and for many, the pandemic became one giant multitasking jumble.

In recent years, many people who never thought of themselves as teachers have gone online and established a following teaching skills as varied as how to apply makeup, make a soufflé, or drive a forklift. YouTube has 1.8 billion monthly users and teaching and learning are one of the most popular uses of the site. More than 85 percent of users say they often use YouTube to learn new things, and seven out of ten say they use YouTube videos for help with work, school, or hobbies.

WRITING IT ALL DOWN TO TEACH

I started my company, Juniper Books, back in the summer of 2001. In the beginning, it was just a hobby focused on buying and selling rare books and first editions one at a time. Then, over the years, I found my niche curating libraries for clients around the world. We put together book collections for everyone from homeowners to interior designers, hotels to real estate developers, and really anyone who wanted their books to be thoughtfully selected and displayed.

"Personal book curator" is not a job title you hear every day but that's essentially what I became. Some people thought I was crazy when I told them about my career. Others wanted to know *how* I did it and if I could share some DIY tips for making their shelves look beautiful.

After I emerged from cancer treatment, I decided to write a book to teach others what I knew about designing and curating a home library. I asked my friend Elizabeth Lane to coauthor the book that eventually became *For the Love of Books: Designing and Curating a Home Library*. Part of the decision to work together was driven by the fact that I needed someone else to help me figure out exactly *what I did, how I did it, and how to teach it to others!*

To write the book and teach the "material," we broke down the overall idea of designing and curating a home library into manageable parts. Sections of the book cover different rooms in a home, and there is DIY advice on how to approach one's shelves. The book teaches our subject matter through written, visual, and kinesthetic methods. Hundreds of photographs of book collections and libraries fill the pages alongside the text.

The experience of slowing down to teach what I knew to others really helped me better understand (and improve) what I do and how to transmit it to my own team at Juniper Books. Writing the book was definitely an exercise in monotasking teaching.

Why Monotasking Teaching Will Help You Do Everything Better

Robert Heinlein, the science fiction author who wrote *Stranger in a Strange Land*, among many other books, reportedly said, "When one teaches, two learn." Teaching will change your life and the lives of those around you—and I don't say that lightly. There are teachers who change the lives of their students every day, not only through the material that they teach, but by connecting with their students and believing in them.

Monotasking teaching helps us master our material. We can monotask teaching just about anything in our lives and we will be smarter and more skilled at whatever we devote our focus to.

Monotasking teaching also strengthens our attention since the task of teaching requires so much focus. Our strengthened attention can then be applied to other parts of our lives—this will make us better at everything we do.

 YOUR TEACHING MONOTASK

Teach Someone to Monotask

For this monotask, you're going to teach someone else to monotask! You can do this in person or on a phone or video call.

- Invite a friend to participate, ideally someone who is open-minded and a good listener.

- Tell your friend that you are reading a self-improvement book and you want to do an exercise with them.

- Inform your friend they may take notes, ask questions, or do anything else that helps them learn what you are teaching.

- Do *not* put away your devices; leave them out in view. The distractions that organically happen will be part of your teaching monotask.

- You can do this task anywhere you wish; in fact, somewhere with a few distractions is helpful.

- Start with an explanation of monotasking—describing it in your own words is part of the task.

- At a certain point, something distracting may happen—one of you may get a notification on your phone, a person will interrupt, or you may see or hear something outside the window. (If you are somewhere distractions are unlikely to happen on their own, set up a timer or alarm before the teaching session that goes off ten minutes after you start).

- Use the distraction as a teachable moment to explain monotasking in action. What should we do when we get distracted? Ask your friend how they would monotask in this situation. Can we gently steer ourselves back to the task and regain our focus?

- At the end of the conversation/monotask, take turns summarizing what you both learned—both about monotasking, and about teaching and learning.

- As a teacher, share how you felt—were you confident? Nervous? Unsure of the material? Did you pick up the book and read a passage from it? Did you share any personal reasons for reading the book and did that help the two of you connect through common purpose?

- Ask your friend to share what they learned and what they thought of your teaching. Did they understand your lesson? Do they want to learn more?

Your Mantra: "Transmit On"

I'll admit that this mantra sounds like a line from *Star Trek*, but given the amazing, almost science fiction-like power of teaching, let's go with it.

Let's transmit our knowledge to others, both for ourselves and for them.

Our teaching can come from a place of good and simply pass on something we know. So *Transmit on.*

The Urge to Multitask

One of the great things about teaching is how difficult it is to multitask while doing it. Like reading, teaching requires your full focus — I consider that a feature, not a flaw. When things are hard to multitask, that means they require effort and attention, which is a good thing. We have to pay attention, bring our full focus to teaching, and then we can do it well.

Do teachers leave their phones on their desk? Do sports coaches answer emails while they are on the field monitoring practice or games? No, professional teachers do one thing at a time. Or at least they should (no one is completely immune to the distractions of modern society).

The urge to multitask will always be real if your devices are within reach or if you have too much going on in your head while you try to teach. It can be hard to concentrate on teaching, especially if you are not used to being in front of people and being somewhat vulnerable in the process.

There is substantial value in sticking with it and turning teaching opportunities into monotasking sessions. If you have an audience, try your best to focus. They are there to learn. You have their attention — use it wisely!

The Reinforcements

You may not always receive validation for teaching from your students — or it may be years later. However, you are having an impact whenever and wherever you teach.

Some reinforcements for your teaching monotask:

Building confidence. If you are confident in your knowledge, and in your ability to teach something, it will definitely help you stay focused while teaching and not get distracted.

Bringing curiosity. If you bring curiosity to your teaching, you will be more relatable as a teacher *and* you will continue learning, both about what you are teaching and the teaching process itself.

Developing empathy. If you can put yourself in the shoes and minds of your learners, then you can adjust your teaching style, your pace, and other factors as needed. Connecting to your students and helping them feel valued, heard, and seen, is as important as what they are learning from you.

The Task in Your Past

When you were younger, did you show a friend how to use a piece of playground equipment, slide faster, or go higher on the swings?

Did you explain to your little brother or sister the rules of a game?

Did you show your parents how to tuck you in at night?

All these are examples of teaching.

Even though we might think we were more often a student than a teacher in our past, there are probably many more examples of teaching in our lives than we realize. When you were getting dressed for a party, or lining up a shot on the basketball court, maybe you had something special you figured out and shared with others and they thought it was pretty cool and started doing it — that was teaching.

When someone asked, "How did you do that?" you showed them. You didn't think about whether you were qualified to teach or whether it was the right moment. You just did it.

And we should do the same thing now.

Amazing Teachers

The tradition of teaching goes back long before schools were formalized or the written word was widely adopted. Indigenous cultures passed on their knowledge to successive generations through stories and other forms of oral transmission. Egyptian hieroglyphs were a visual form of writing that told stories and provided instructions, including teaching the dead how to advance in the afterlife.

One of the most famous teachers in the ancient world was Socrates, the Greek philosopher. It is from him that we have the Socratic method—a way of asking questions in order to teach and learn. He said, "The most that can be done is that one person who is more knowledgeable than another can, by asking a series of questions, stimulate the other to think, and so cause him to learn for himself."

History is full of other amazing teachers. Booker T. Washington was born into slavery and went on to develop Tuskegee Institute in Alabama. Annie Sullivan, a graduate of a school for the blind, taught Helen Keller when she was a child by spelling out words into her hand. Jaime Escalante, an East Los Angeles math teacher featured in the movie *Stand and Deliver*, helped record numbers of students pass the Advanced Placement Calculus exam when no one else believed in them. Frank McCourt taught in New York City schools for twenty-seven years and wrote the best-selling memoirs *Angela's Ashes* and *Teacher Man*.

MY MOST MEMORABLE TEACHERS

I've had many teachers in my life, but these three stand out for having a big impact on me:

My father. My father taught himself to cook after he left his law practice. Over seventeen years in the restaurant business, he transmitted his creative and somewhat revolutionary ideas to dozens of chefs at the Quilted Giraffe. Many of those chefs later went on to open their own restaurants, win awards, write cookbooks, and accomplish other great things. He may not have the qualities of a traditional classroom teacher — he can get impatient and frustrated when ideas that are super clear to him are not quickly understood by other people — but he is an effective teacher. He taught me how to hold a knife properly, how to make mashed potato sushi, and how to keep creating all the time and not worry about what other people think about what you are doing.

My yoga teacher. I took a yoga teacher training course in my twenties with my favorite instructor, Shiva Rea. I really liked her regular yoga classes and while I had no intention of teaching yoga, I was hungry to learn more and deepen my practice. When it came time to demonstrate a pose in front of the class — most of whom did plan to teach yoga — I got pretty flustered. Like a great teacher, Shiva didn't hang me out to dry; she casually made a joke and brought the attention of the class back to learning. It was good for me to get out of my comfort zone.

My first art professor. My first art class in college was Basic Design, in my junior year. I loved that the class was experiential — we were given assignments and each student came up with something completely different. For one project the professor, Louise Hamlin, saved her critique of my work for last after reviewing the work of about fifteen other students. I was a little worried (and sleepy from having pulled an all-nighter). I had painstakingly collected hundreds of autumn leaves from around campus, then glued them into a collage that followed the transition of fall colors in New England. Professor Hamlin's comments were so encouraging about the originality of my project that I took a studio art class every semester thereafter and years later established a career in design and the visual arts.

How You'll Know You're Good at It

You'll know you are good at monotasking teaching when:

- You can stop at a moment's notice and teach what you are doing to someone if they ask you. Approaching life with the ability to teach what you are doing is powerful, as it requires you to pay attention more of the time.

- You seek out feedback from others. Whether you are teaching in real life or online, don't be afraid to ask your students how you are doing. This comes with some risk as you may receive critical feedback. Listen, don't be discouraged, find the constructive comments, and make changes from there.

- You seek out great teachers and learn something from them. Sign up for an offering from MasterClass, or a MOOC (a Massive Online Open Class). Or observe teaching in its pure form, without a slick audiovisual production—consider a continuing education class or attend a lecture at your local library or museum. I love watching and listening to vintage recordings of great teachers, including the Feynman Lectures on Physics or Alan Watts and his talks on Eastern philosophy and human consciousness.

- You try your hand at making a video or writing a post about something you know how to do—even if you don't share it. Record your own TED Talk that you might give or write up how-to instructions on any topic. Even if you don't have an audience, pretending like you do have one helps us formalize our approach and thoughts.

What if...

...*you're not an expert in anything?* Whatever interests you has the potential to be interesting to others. Figure out what you love and teach someone about it.

...*you don't want to be a teacher?* While you certainly don't have to teach, it's rare to go through life without needing to explain something to someone or taking the opportunity to show someone how to do something. You can teach by example. The passengers in your car will see that you signal your turns and obey traffic laws—that's teaching. The person behind you in line at the post office will see you being polite to the clerk at the counter—that's teaching. Your friend may see you cooking something and notice how you did it and how wonderfully it turned out—that's teaching. A child may see you changing a tire on your bicycle and watch the steps you do—that's teaching. A random stranger may see you patiently correcting your dog on a walk—that's teaching.

...*you don't have the confidence to stand in front of others?* Unless your job requires it, you don't need to stand in front of others (although if you do need to, you may surprise yourself and find that you like it). Teaching doesn't have to be something organized or intentional—you can teach someone simply by living your life and by doing what you do.

Go Teach!

This is a monotask that you can either do spontaneously, or with preparation. Whatever you do, give it your full attention!

There are at least ninety-nine things you can teach right now. How to walk a dog. How to brush your teeth. How to make toast. You can teach in person, make a video, or write it down. Have fun and stay focused.

TASK 9: PLAYING

'll be honest, I have not always been great at making time to play. Sometimes I take life too seriously and, very often, I work too hard. Since my experience with cancer and chemotherapy a few years ago, I have made a much bigger effort to relax and play on a regular basis. I know that life is short and living a balanced life is important.

My friend Ed is a lot better at playing than me. We went to college together decades ago and meet up about once a year now to ski and see a concert or two—that's just a small slice of the playing that Ed does year-round. Before the pandemic put live concerts on hold, Ed went to at least a hundred shows a year. From my perspective, he always seemed to be traveling, having fun, and playing outdoors!

It wasn't always this way. Ed spent the first few years after college working around the clock in the finance industry. Living in New York City, he watched many colleagues spend two to three hours a day commuting to work, then put in long stressful days, all in the pursuit of making more money for clients and themselves.

In 2001, after some of his colleagues lost their lives at the World Trade Center on September 11, Ed decided to adjust his priorities and live life to the fullest. He realized that life was not about making as much money as possible, doing what other people wanted him to do, or doing what society expected of him. Since then he's spent more time skiing, taken up kiteboarding, and really gotten into the music scene—all while working in the medical field and starting a family.

Ed's advice for those who say they don't have the money or time to play is to get creative. If you want to go to a music festival but can't afford it, volunteer to work the festival. If you plan on working now and saving your playtime for later in life, consider how precious life is—carve out time to do the things that make you happy, spend time with friends, travel, and experience new things.

I've learned a lot from Ed over the years about making play a more regular part of my life. Play definitely makes me a happier and more productive person.

Let's jump into our playing monotask and have some fun exploring the joy and benefits of play.

The Facts About Playing

We live in stressful times. Do we simply work too hard? Is there enough time left in the day/week/year to play? Quality of life means different things to different people, but throughout human history, leisure time to pursue your hobbies, unwind, relax, and play has been important. Compared to Europeans, Americans tend to focus more on work and financial success rather than quality of life. We work about four hundred hours more per year than our counterparts in countries such as Denmark, Norway, and Germany.

From a young age in the U.S., kids are pushed to work hard, compete, and succeed. The U.S. Department of Health and Human Services recommends one hour of physical activity daily for children. In comparison, in Finland the recommendation is three.

Anthony D. Pellegrini, PhD, the author of *Recess: Its Role in Education and Development* and emeritus professor of educational psychology at the University of Minnesota, found in all his experiments involving children in elementary school that students paid better attention after a break than before. "Recess is... associated with improved classroom behavior and attention. Research demonstrates that fidgeting increases prior to recess, especially when recess is delayed for a longer period of time," Dr. Pellegrini and coauthor Catherine M. Bohn-Gettler, PhD, wrote in their article "The Benefits of Recess in Primary School."

Play is good for us as children, and it's good for us as adults. Many hardworking American adults try to cram their playtime into an occasional vacation, then go back to work. Play is not something you should bottle up and release only once a year or every few years when you get around to taking a vacation.

WHEN PLAY IS NO LONGER PLAYFUL

I first got into mountain biking in college and it quickly became my favorite form of play. Wherever I lived, and often when I traveled, I would mountain bike on local trails.

A couple decades later, when I was nearing forty, a friend suggested that I try racing. It seemed like it could be a good way to stay in shape and spend more time outside doing something I loved, so I decided to give it a try. I signed up for some local mountain bike races in Colorado and soon discovered how serious the competition was. To keep up and have any chance of getting on the podium, I'd have to start training seriously and work on my bike-handling skills. Soon I was entering races every week, plus I added cyclocross, a very fun, but also very fast-paced and intense form of bike racing, to my schedule.

It wasn't long before I signed up with a coach to help me formalize my training program. He put together a schedule that required me to ride about ten to twelve hours a week, including some tough interval training sessions. While my fitness improved and I achieved better race results, I was exhausted *all* the time.

I had inadvertently turned my playtime into a source of stress. Riding had become more of a chore than something I did for fun. It no longer had all the benefits that biking for play provided. Eventually, I "retired" from my mediocre racing career and returned to riding bikes just for play.

Now I ride with my kids, with friends, or by myself. It's nice to be fit so I try to stay in shape, but mostly I enjoy being outdoors and having fun.

Why Monotasking Playing Will Help You Do Everything Better

Now, more than ever, we all need to rest and recharge, and play is one of the most effective ways we can reset our bodies and our brains. Through play, we can get away from work physically and mentally.

We've often been taught that if we truly want to get somewhere in our lives, we have to work hard and stay focused on our goals. But what if the best way to get from Point A to Point B is to detour to rest stops much more frequently?

Everyone thinks work has to be all serious, that you can only meet in a conference room or over coffee. Work meetings can, and should, happen in places that inspire creativity and different ways of thinking — at the park, or a museum, for example — and include activities that get us out of our heads and away from our stress. A class at Stanford called "From Play to Innovation" is all about integrating play at work to fuel creativity and innovation.

There is also a common perception that play for adults equals sports. Play can be anything that takes your mind off everyday life and keeps it there while you reset, alleviating your anxiety and bringing you joy. Good old-fashioned board games are one way to do this—they have grown in popularity in recent years with a multitude of new games being launched, and classics becoming top sellers again.

David Sax writes about analog gaming—as compared to video gaming—in *The Revenge of Analog: Real Things and Why They Matter*, explaining, "With analog gaming, whether it is an intricate board game or a child's game of tag, all the players need to work together to create the illusion of the game. It requires a collective investment of your imagination in an alternate reality to believe that you actually own Park Avenue, and the colored slips of paper in your hands are worth something." The benefits that come from monotasking your analog play—including developing focus, collaborating with others, and releasing your stress—are transferable to other parts of life.

If we work all the time, we get in a rut. We tend to become burned out, anxious, and depressed. When we make time for play, we can return to work or school or our creative pursuits refreshed and rejuvenated. Play is not a new invention, but in our fast-paced, overscheduled world, we need to remind ourselves to play, and may need to invent ways to play again.

 YOUR PLAYING MONOTASK

Don't Think, Just Play

For this task, you get to play! I'm going to leave it up to you to decide what sort of play.

If you already have a sport or a hobby you enjoy, feel free to do that. But take a new, playful approach. If you're a runner, maybe try skipping during your run. If you're a swimmer, get a float to relax, or jump into the pool like a kid.

For this task, try not to choose an activity such as chess that requires a lot of thinking, or anything extremely sedentary like working on a puzzle. Also, for now, avoid video games and anything that requires a device. These are all forms of play that you can return to later. The ideal setting for this monotask is outdoors where you can move your body and feel the wind in your face.

If you're in the city, go to the park. If you have kids, take them along. If you have a backyard, turn the sprinklers on and run through them. Don't worry about what you look like playing, just play.

If you haven't played or moved your body in a while, start with something reasonable — you don't want to hurt yourself.

Now to get started:

- Set aside at least twenty minutes to play, plus any time you need to get to and from your play area, and clean-up time.

- Choose something you love to do or have wanted to do for a while.

- Set yourself up with whatever you need for this activity: a bicycle, a basketball, your dog. You're welcome to play with a friend; just make sure they know this is not a serious workout and you won't be talking about the office. If the conversation requires you to think, then no talking is best.

- Clear your mind and enjoy what you are doing.

- If you start thinking about work, life, or anything stressful, acknowledge that thought and let it go. Don't judge yourself — it happens to everyone and we can work on becoming less distracted while we play over time.

- Be present and in the moment with your full body, mind, and soul.

- Relax into how good it feels to be immersed in something completely. Let everything else in life melt away.

- Smile. Laugh out loud.

- Tell yourself "I should do this more often."

If your chosen activity isn't fun for you, try something else. There are so many ways to play, and so many benefits. See the sidebar in this chapter for more ideas, and also check out monotasking.tips.

Your Mantra: "Play Away"

You might be going through an immensely challenging or depressing time of life. But if you get out of your everyday routine and play for a while, it can make a big difference and help you play your stress away.

Remind yourself to have fun by using the mantra *Play away* — play does take you away to a good place.

The Urge to Multitask

Play is most fun and effective when we can really immerse ourselves in it.

While you are playing, ideally you will be able to monotask without thinking about it. However, if you experience multitasking temptations and find it hard to resist them, consider exploring other forms of play that might better limit your distractions and help you fully engage with play. Choose something that is ridiculously fun, so much so that you don't want to do anything else at the same time.

Most outdoor play activities allow for greater immersion and fewer interruptions than indoor options, but distractions still exist. While theoretically you can multitask on your phone while running, biking, hiking, fishing, and doing similar activities, I recommend resisting that urge. Once you know what it feels like to be engaged in play on its own, you can selectively add back music, podcasts, and other background tasks.

No matter what, you should enjoy your playtime — don't work while playing!

The Reinforcements

The reinforcements for keeping your adult life playful are not too complicated or burdensome. It can be as simple as a word, a memory, or freeing up a little time.

In *Joyful: The Surprising Power of Ordinary Things to Create Extraordinary Happiness*, Ingrid Fetell Lee says, "I've found that just saying the word 'treehouse' causes people to smile, no matter their age. It is like a password to the inner child's sanctum, a place both exotic and familiar, a place of memories and dreams."

What is your "treehouse"? Keep your senses open to discovering the magical word, place, or smell that transports you to a state of relaxation and playfulness.

If you didn't have to work to earn a living, would you just play all day? Or would that get boring after a while? For most people, playing all the time might get, well, a bit monotonous! Be sure to keep play special and fun, not something you feel obligated to do.

Some people get caught up in posting on social media about how great their lives are. Then they feel like they have to keep up an image even at times when it may not be true (we all have our ups and downs). Play because you want to and it gives you joy, not because others have gotten used to seeing and hearing about how great your life is.

Other reinforcements include playing with others if possible. We can bond and connect with friends and family through play. When we are all relaxed and having fun it's different than spending time with someone at work, at a conference, or in a formal setting.

Having a regular schedule for play is also great to make sure you get your playtime in. It's so easy in life to fill up the time with "important" tasks, but setting aside time to play might mean scheduling a casual weekend bike ride, a summer trip, or a social event that is truly fun and not just an obligation.

Overall, being present in the moment will be so enjoyable that you will want to get back there as much as possible, and you can find your way there easily through play.

The Task in Your Past

What were some of the happiest days of your life? If you were to make a list of the top ten days when you were the happiest, what would they be?

For me, one of those days would be the first day I went skiing. I was nine years old and I remember being exhilarated. Everything was so new and exciting—the feeling of speeding down the slopes of Hunter Mountain was something I could not get enough of. Since then, many of the happiest days on my top ten list as an adult have also been on the ski slopes (now mostly in Colorado where I'm very fortunate to live).

You may have childhood memories of playing basketball on the neighborhood court, softball in the backyard, going roller-skating, swimming, or just climbing a tree. Maybe you remember crafting on a rainy day, getting really involved in completing a puzzle, or making up a game with a friend. Perhaps you have good memories of a specific trip where you were especially carefree.

That child loved to play and so do you.

Famous Players!

Professional athletes get paid to play for a living. There are some — Michael Jordan on the basketball court, Alex Morgan on the soccer pitch, and Roger Federer on the tennis court, come to mind — who are so good at what they do that they make it look easy and fun.

Some would describe this as being in a state of "flow." Mihaly Csikszentmihalyi, PhD, a psychologist and author of *Flow: the Psychology of Optimal Experience*, defines flow as "a state in which people are so involved in an activity that nothing else seems to matter; the experience is so enjoyable that people will continue to do it even at great cost, for the sheer sake of doing it." Flow is something that we can strive for with all of our monotasking; play may be one of the first places we can achieve it.

Outside of their work, many athletes and celebrities find various ways to play. David Beckham first got into Lego while recovering from an Achilles tendon injury and bought a nearly six-thousand-piece Taj Mahal set to pass the time. Years later, playing with Lego was one of the ways he stayed busy while quarantining in 2020. He said of his playtime, "I think Lego sometimes helps to calm me down."

In their spare time, actor Will Smith enjoys fencing, actress Leslie Mann rides a unicycle, and Susan Sarandon loves to play ping-pong. The hobbies of well-known people often inspire new playtime passions among their fans. Everyone plays, or should play, at least some of the time!

PLAYTIME STARTER LIST

Play is anything you do that gives you joy. It doesn't need to have a goal, except play in itself. It can include sports: playing catch, tennis, or paddle boarding. It can also be improv comedy, painting, or a round of Trivial Pursuit. Maybe it's shooting pool, or just lounging around the pool. Here are a few more ideas to play with!

1. Go to the park, kick a soccer ball, throw a ball, or toss a Frisbee.
2. Take the afternoon off at the beach or on the water: boating, kayaking, tubing, canoeing, or another activity.
3. Go for a bike ride.
4. Go for a hike in the mountains.
5. Take the day off and go skiing, snowboarding, or snowshoeing.
6. Go bowling, miniature golfing, or do something similar that you haven't done in a while.
7. Go to a concert, sing out loud, and as the saying goes, dance like no one is watching.
8. Throw a party, a really fun one.
9. Play with your pets, get on the floor with them.
10. Dress up! Wear a costume, a fancy outfit, or something outrageous.
11. Play cards or a board game.
12. Read a book to your kids and really act it out with silly voices and funny sounds.

How You'll Know You're Good at It

The goal of monotasking play is not about getting in shape or becoming particularly skilled at a hobby or sport. If that happens, it's great, but the real purpose is to have fun, relieve stress, and be refreshed when you get back to everything else you need to do. You'll know you are good at monotasking playing when:

* You make time to play on a regular basis.
* You get creative about playing while on business trips, when you are really busy, when the weather is bad, and in other situations where you have to expend a little more energy to get your playtime in.
* You are happier and less anxious.
* You are able to lose yourself in play, not thinking about work or your to-do list.
* You seek out friends who want to play like you do.
* You develop deeper connections with your children through play.

What if...

...you're physically limited or have a disability? Play is not only about sports or physical activity. There are many other ways to play, from card games to making music, seeing a live show, drawing, making crafts, and more.

...you truly don't have time to play? Make time in small increments, even sixty seconds or a few minutes. Play on the way to work. Take a break from work to play; it really will help you do your work better.

...you're a busy parent and playing with your kids is your only option? I've been there. I've been exhausted. I've gotten bored of doing what my kids want to do instead of what I want. Children

grow up quickly and while they are young, they are the most fun people on the planet! Appreciate the fact that you don't really need to teach children to play—they instinctively know how to do it, and they can drop into play nearly instantaneously.

...*you feel guilty playing?* Everyone deserves time to play. Make time for yourself, and if you can help others make time for themselves, do so in any way you can. Contribute or volunteer with organizations that help get kids outside, build trails, clean up playgrounds, work with disabled athletes, or do other good things in the world.

Go Play!

Go have some fun. You deserve a break.

TASK 10: SEEING

took my dog, Maple, for a walk recently on a beautiful trail in Colorado. At the trailhead, there was a poster board-sized sign with a menacing photo of a snake and a written warning about rattlesnakes on the trail. Scary, right?

I made some mental calculations about the risk of actually encountering a rattlesnake and figured I would take my chances, so I proceeded with the hike. Maple was on a leash and I kept her close by. We started down the path and were enjoying a relaxing stroll when a park ranger showed up.

At first, I thought there had been a new snake sighting and he was clearing hikers off the trail. Much to my surprise, he was there to write me a $75 ticket for having a dog on the trail.

I explained the honest truth—that I was distracted by the giant rattlesnake warning poster at the trailhead. I had not seen the much smaller *no dogs* sign a few feet away—next to about ten other signs.

The ranger wasn't buying my "I was distracted by the big sign" defense. I even reenacted how I had approached the trail, my curiosity piqued by the shiny rattlesnake poster visible from the parking lot. I showed how it pulled me (and probably most other visitors) toward it, passing by all the tiny signs on the way without even a glance.

He stood firm and explained that it was my responsibility to read all the signs and follow the rules. Fair enough—I've read and obeyed plenty of *no biking* and *no camping* signs over the years. The point I was trying to make was that the rattlesnake sign was too good—it was overly effective at attracting people's attention. Yes, everyone would know about the rattlesnake danger and be cautious, but they might unknowingly break all the other rules. The ranger wasn't interested in discussing my theories about visual distractions and the attention economy—he handed me a ticket and sent me on my way.

Life is like that a lot of times. We don't see *everything* that is in our field of view for many reasons. Sometimes it's because we only see what other people want us to see—they direct our attention. Other times it's because we create our own tunnel vision—we choose not to see it all.

Our eyes are the portal into our brains for most of the information that we take in. Those who profit from our attention—including advertisers, media companies, and app designers—know this, and so there are a lot of forces vying for our eyeballs at all times.

Internally, we are aware, at least subconsciously, that we can't take in everything all the time. We limit ourselves by choosing what to see and what not to see. Sometimes, the seeing habits we've developed over years create a form of visual bias—we don't see everything, and we make judgments about what we are seeing without necessarily knowing it. These judgments may include thoughts about what is important, relevant, attractive, dangerous, and more.

Our seeing monotask is all about balancing the choice between focusing on one thing with all of our attention and broadening our vision to see everything that is out there.

The Facts About Seeing

We all see a lot of ads every day. It's nearly impossible to avoid them. In the 1970s, the average American was exposed to about five hundred ads a day between billboards, television, radio, and print. Today, digital marketing experts estimate that the number is closer to ten thousand ads per day—and those ads are increasingly "micro-targeted" to us based on a huge amount of data that companies possess about our habits and interests.

The growth of advertising in recent decades has come mostly from internet ads. At first the ads appeared in the same places—on the side of a Google search page or on a website that rented out a portion of its space to make money, but now they're pretty much everywhere. Advertising revenue has built some of the biggest businesses on the planet including Google, YouTube (owned by Google), Facebook, and Instagram (owned by Facebook). Even Amazon generates substantial revenue from advertising fees paid by Amazon vendors and sellers who want the best exposure for their products.

We can't possibly see ten thousand ads a day and process them all. Advertisers have to get more creative about how to get our attention. Their goal is to create ads that we really do "see," and ideally take action from. Once we get used to one type of ad, we might tune them out, so advertisers work to capture our eyeballs (and our wallets) in new and different ways.

Our eyes are exhausted from all that we are seeing. Being exposed to five hundred ads each day would be tiring but seeing twenty times that number really wears us down in ways that most of us can probably feel but can't quite pinpoint.

In the future we are likely to be exposed to even more visual stimulation. In order to process everything around us, we have to take back control of our attention. Let's start by monotasking seeing.

Some of My Favorite Sights

It is a wonderful feeling to see things that make us happy. Do you get a smile on your face and does your stress melt away when you see certain people, places, or things? Here are some of the sights that I love:

- My children's smiling faces
- My dog, Maple, sleeping peacefully
- The sun setting over Longs Peak in Rocky Mountain National Park, visible from my backyard
- The New York City skyline at night
- The night skies over Saint-Rémy-de-Provence, in France, just as van Gogh saw them
- Going deep into a forest and seeing nothing but trees in every direction
- Turning over a rock and seeing an entire universe of life underneath
- Large snowflakes falling outside as seen from a cozy indoor couch
- Lush green hills in springtime, just about anywhere
- A beautiful library or bookstore, especially one with a library ladder!

Why Monotasking Seeing Will Help You Do Everything Better

We all know the value of sight. Our eyes help us navigate and make sense of the world. We can see danger, beautiful things, people we know, their facial expressions, and body language.

Monotasking seeing helps us focus on *details* that may get lost in the visual clutter of our lives.

Monotasking seeing also helps us understand *context*.

Monotasking seeing can help us see complexity, nuance, and subtleties. When we monotask seeing, we can better recognize that things are not often as they seem, and we can look further and think more deeply about what we are seeing.

At an even more basic level, in our highly overstimulated world, monotasking seeing can help us turn down the dial on what we are exposed to. In *The World Beyond Your Head: On Becoming an Individual in an Age of Distraction*, Matthew B. Crawford explains, "Our changing technological environment generates a need for ever more stimulation. The content of the stimulation almost becomes irrelevant. Our distractibility seems to indicate that we are agnostic on the question of what is worth paying attention to—that is, what to value."

 YOUR SEEING MONOTASK

SEE LESS TO SEE MORE

The idea of your seeing monotask is to limit what you take in visually so that you can better appreciate what you do see.

- Set aside twenty minutes.

- Turn off notifications on your phone, put it away, or leave it behind.

- Put on comfortable shoes and go for a walk.

- This task is different from your walking monotask — this walk is about your eyes. Your feet and your body know what to do; let them do their thing. Focus on your eyes and seeing with this task.

- Almost every walk will have enough visual variety for this monotask, so don't worry too much about where you go.

- As you walk, look at objects at different distances — three feet, twelve feet, a hundred feet, a mile away, as far as you can see. What do you see?

- Look up at the sky and clouds, treetops, buildings, birds flying. Make a mental note of what you see, the variety and the details. Consider for a moment what you *would* take a picture of, but then let that thought go and return to seeing with only your eyes.

- Look down at the ground, the grass, the pavement, at your feet moving steadily. Consider the differences between objects you see that are fixed in place and those that are in motion. What do you see that is different about them? Do you notice one type more than the other?

- Look into the distance as far as you can see. What is there?

- Focus on something you can just barely see or something mysterious, and try to discern what it is: a sign, an animal, a piece of junk in a field? Perhaps it is something temporary or ephemeral — maybe an alignment of objects at different distances?

- Consider what you are seeing for the *first* time. If you are on one of your usual routes, what have you noticed that is new for you? Was it there all along?

- Consider what you might be seeing for the *last* time.

- Think about whether your other senses help you see.

- Think about whether your previous experience helps you see, or gets in the way of your seeing. Your expectations may guide your understanding of what you *think* you are seeing; question whether that is actually so.

- Actively try to look for something you don't like. Was it there all along and you didn't want to see it? It could be your least favorite color, pollution, incoming weather, a sign for a business you're not fond of, or a person doing something while they think no one is watching.

- Reflect on the experience of seeing without screens. What you saw was not someone else's version of life put onto a screen for you to consume. How does it make you feel to see only with your eyes? How does it make you feel to see what is out there in the real world?

Your Mantra: "See Near and Far"

While there are a lot of good mantras we could use to focus our seeing monotask, I've come up with one that I think is helpful for our current times.

See near and far reminds us to take breaks from all the "near" seeing we do—looking at screens a few inches in front of our faces.

When we look "far"—across the room, out the window, at the mountains, over the ocean—our vision becomes more expansive.

Then we can return to looking near, but remind ourselves to look at more than our devices. The details of nature, architecture, and other objects right in front of us are truly fascinating.

The Urge to Multitask

Since the only time we essentially "turn off" our eyes is when we sleep (about one-third of our day), we ask a lot of our eyes during the other two-thirds of the day. In the approximately sixteen hours that our eyes are open, there are a lot of people and companies who want you to look at them.

Your eyes are where an advertiser will start the process of getting you to pay attention to what they want you to pay attention to. The advertising posts in your Twitter or Facebook feed are designed to distract you from the reason you are probably there (to get updates from your friends, colleagues, and other people you follow). TV commercials, billboards, neon signs—they have all become increasingly loud and attention grabbing. Try to stay focused on what you came to see, not what others want you to see.

As you progress with your monotasking skills, you will become much more aware of when you are monotasking and when you are multitasking, as well as when others are trying to distract you. Try to limit what you see and as a result where your attention goes.

The Reinforcements

There are a lot of ways to reinforce your seeing monotask.

Looking for and being able to see fine details will encourage you to look for more.

Stepping back and seeing the big picture will help you understand context, meaning, and relationships.

Seeing beautiful things can be addictive in a healthy way — you will want to travel more, see new places, and perhaps what you may have taken for granted will become beautiful in a new light. Seeing things you have never seen, or that you don't see every day, will reinforce your ability to see with more of your attention.

Seeing all of humanity and seeing the world from the perspective of others helps reinforce the amazing powers of sight that we share. You can see how large the world is and yet we are all in this together.

Recording what you see through photography can capture your unique view of the world and be a great way to help others see the world through your eyes. Once you've practiced monotasking seeing, you can choose when to take photos — not of everything and every moment; instead, focus on what is truly special to photograph. First use your eyes to see, then selectively use your phone.

Describing what you see in a journal can capture details or the essence of what you saw. Writing will help you think and reflect on what you saw, put it in context, and consider its meaning.

Anticipation will help reinforce your monotask as well. The more you see, the more you will want to see.

The Task in Your Past

When babies are born, they can typically only focus on objects eight to twelve inches in front of them. Their eye muscles strengthen and improve quickly so that they can see and take in more of the world through their eyes.

I find it somewhat ironic that most of the human race now spends so much time staring at objects — phones and tablets — eight to twelve inches in front of our faces. Perhaps we all just want to return to our childhood?

In all seriousness, there was a time in our younger years when life was simple. After we came out of the womb, we saw our parents. Later we saw our food and toys. We were amazing monotaskers at a young age! We pretty much did not notice *anything* that did not satisfy our immediate needs.

At some point, we started using our eyes to do amazing things like reading and learning. Maybe we watched someone else do a dance or a sport, then imitated it. We started to notice more of the world beyond our immediate environment the first time we visited a city, or saw a mountain, or an incredible sunset.

The process that we all go through of growing up and using our eyes is incredible when you think about it. But it can also be overwhelming because there is so much to take in. It's nice to think back to the simplicity of our early months and years, when we didn't see everything—we saw one thing at a time and it was everything to us. And that was monotasking.

Amazing Vision

Humans have long sought to understand the world and our place in it. Throughout history, we have taken in enormous amounts of information through our eyes about weather, terrain, wildlife, and people.

The ability to see helps us survive, and in many communities, seeing more than what others see has been highly prized. The Sān people of Southern Africa have developed exceptional tracking skills in the Kalahari Desert for tens of thousands of years. When one's life, and the life of an entire community, depends on *seeing* to find food and shelter, it becomes a monotask. Reading the landscape, observing the weather, identifying animal tracks—all of these actions require one to bring their full attention to what they see, and make sense of it.

In recent years, advances in satellite technology and machine learning have enabled the outsourcing of our eyes to computers that can look at images faster and detect more than the human eye. While this is impressive and helpful for many areas of research and science, we should still use our eyes when we can.

Clearly the monotask of seeing is connected to other monotasks, covered in other chapters, such as creating, thinking, learning, walking, and reading. These tasks often start with our ability to see in a clear and focused manner.

SEEING THE SOCCER FIELD

My son loves soccer — playing, watching, and refereeing the game. The day that he turned twelve and became eligible, he registered for referee training. A few weeks later he was out on the field refereeing games for kids younger than him.

For years, even before he started working as a referee, he had a really good understanding of the rules of the game and had a great eye for spotting fouls, understanding and making offside calls, and determining if a goal was really a goal — which can be harder than it looks! We watched a lot of soccer on TV and he would constantly ask me questions like "Do you think he was offside?" and "Do you think that deserved a yellow or red card?" I could rarely see what he saw, even with the slow-motion replays — but he was almost always right about the call.

I asked my son what it takes to be a good referee and how he's able to see the whole field at once — even for youth soccer, the fields are pretty big. He said he stays very focused and consistent, and doesn't get bothered when players, parents, or coaches try to distract or sway him. He has picked up some tactics from more experienced referees, such as anticipating where the next play will be so he will be in a better position to see the action.

By the time he'd refereed a few dozen games, he had become good at pattern recognition. He knows the types of calls he'll have to make when refereeing different age groups (for example, older players are more physical and commit more fouls). This way he's trained himself to look for certain things and then he can act quickly and decisively when he sees them.

How You'll Know You're Good at It

When you make progress at monotasking seeing, you'll find that you can control what you are seeing much better. You'll be able to make sense of what you see without being overwhelmed by everything *others* want you to see. You will know you are good at monotasking seeing when:

- You can tune out visual distractions.
- You want to tell someone about the amazing things you see.
- You go to a concert or other live experience and can be fully present. You could take a picture, but you find that experiencing it with your eyes (and other senses) is the best way to be in the moment.
- You see better while doing other monotasks, such as getting there/driving. Once you can do one task with your full focus, you will be better able to combine tasks as needed.
- You use other senses to make sense of the world. When you develop the ability to see with focus and comprehend what you are seeing, your other senses such as touching, hearing, and smelling, might improve.

- You direct your newfound control of your eyes to find love, food, shelter, and other important things in life.
- Perhaps, most of all, you see without trying too hard. The more you practice monotasking, the more seeing clearly will come naturally.

What if...

...*you have a vision impairment?* There are ways to "see" using your other senses, which the blind community does every day to experience the world. A visual picture of the world around us can be formed by using a combination of sound, smell, taste, and touch. Putting any or all of these senses to use in order to see the world is a worthy monotask to explore.

...*you think you've seen it all?* Change your focus—look near *and* far. Look through a microscope, look through a telescope. There is way more to see than anyone can view in their lifetime.

...*you think there is nothing to see where you are?* Stop using your brain and open your eyes! There is a lot to see if you look. Take a trip to shake things up and see something new. Then practice seeing near and far when you get home.

...*you have a smartphone in front of your face all the time?* Put it down, hide it, leave it behind. Go for a walk around the block without it. Use your eyes, not your phone, to experience the world.

Go See!

Put down this book and go see something you've never seen.

Take a walk. Look around. I'll see you (ha ha) in the next chapter.

TASK 11: CREATING

My definition of creativity is pretty broad: bringing anything into the world that did not previously exist. Whether you decide intentionally to create something ("I'm going to write a song") or it just happens as part of your day ("I figured out how to get to work on time!"), creating is fun, and can be beneficial for your life and that of others. While not everyone considers themselves to be creative, we all create on a daily basis even if we don't call it that.

For some people, and at some times, the pressure to be creative is helpful in order to create, while for other people and at other times it can be counterproductive to creativity. Howard Gardner, PhD, is a psychologist and the author of *Creating Minds: An Anatomy of Creativity as Seen Through the Lives of Freud, Einstein, Picasso, Stravinsky, Eliot, Graham, and Gandhi*. In his book he writes, "Indeed, knowledge that one will be judged on some criterion of 'creativeness' or 'originality' tends to narrow the scope of what one can produce (leading to products that are then judged as relatively conventional); in contrast, the absence of an evaluation seems to liberate creativity."

We can be very creative now thanks to advances in technology and communications that not only power our creativity, but also expand the ways in which we can share it. I've repeatedly called out our phones and devices as sources of distraction and multitasking temptation throughout this book, but when it comes to creating, they can come in very handy.

Not only can we *create* on electronic devices—writing, drawing, taking pictures, making movies—but we can also learn *how* to be more creative using apps, watching tutorials, and seeking inspiration from other creators. Further, we can share our creations with a global audience if we so choose—not only through the most popular social media platforms, but also through thousands of sites dedicated to creative communities.

Whether you are motivated by creating for money, achieving fame, improving your home life, or something else, there is a lot to be said for working on your creativity. Isolating creating as a monotask is a great place to start.

The Facts About Creating

There is a phenomenal amount of creative activity happening every day in every corner of the globe. This can be seen on the big online platforms that host a sizable amount of creativity. More than 100 million photos are posted to Instagram *per day* according to Omnicore. YouTube reports that its videos are watched for 1 billion hours daily. Etsy boasts of 4.3 million active sellers, mostly small creators.

Apple has historically been one of the most creative companies in the technology industry, both in terms of their product innovation and their alignment with artists and creators. Their 1997 advertising featured this narration: "Here's to the crazy ones, the misfits, the rebels, the troublemakers, the round pegs in the square holes...the ones who see things differently—they're not fond of rules..." The implied promise of this ad was that individuals who buy and use Apple computers would also create, innovate, and change the world. Indeed, Apple technology has enabled a substantial amount of creativity in recent decades.

The growth in self-publishing, 3D printing, and crowdfunding also reflects the healthy state of the creative world. There were 1.68 million books self-published in 2018 and 3D printing is a $10 billion market. Successful crowdfunded projects on sites including Kickstarter and Indiegogo have raised money to design and manufacture watches, furniture, and clothing, make movies, publish illustrated books, and fund museums. Raising money for a creative idea is a creative endeavor in itself that requires a lot of monotasking to reach a successful outcome. Marketing your idea, and yourself (personal branding, influencer marketing, and whatever the next buzzword may be), are also creative pursuits.

CATCHING CREATIVE IDEAS

Sometimes great ideas come to me while I'm biking, walking, driving, or doing something else. I don't set out to create when I'm doing these things; that would be multitasking. The creativity just happens in the background.

Other times, ideas emerge during dedicated creative time at my desk or when I'm writing in my journal. At these times, I am deliberately monotasking. Overall, it's hard to predict when creative ideas will arrive — I just have to be ready to catch them.

I have a notebook for ideas that I keep separate from my writing journal. It contains all sorts of ideas for stories, novels, screenplays, new businesses, new products, marketing strategies, and more. Sometimes an idea will graduate from the ideas notebook to having its own Google doc. In there, I'll develop concepts further, and quite often unite a bunch of disparate thoughts into one overall project.

I'm not as protective of my ideas as I once was; sometimes creative ideas need to be exposed to the light to grow. Occasionally I keep an idea to myself for a really long time (or forever), and other times, I seek out feedback in order to determine if it's a good idea, or to evolve it.

Monotasking creating has helped me understand how best to nurture my creativity. The attention I've given to my own creative process has resulted in more ideas, and improved my ability to turn the best ideas into reality.

Why Monotasking Creating Will Help You Do Everything Better

In *The Artist's Way*, Julia Cameron inspired millions of readers to make time to be creative in part or all of their life. "No matter what your age or your life path, whether making art is your career or your hobby or your dream," she wrote, "it is not too late or too egotistical or too selfish or too silly to work on your creativity."

Creating something—a painting, a garden, a computer program—of any size can help us improve our thinking and our enjoyment of life. You don't need to create something huge.

Here are some ways that monotasking creating can help you do everything better. At the very least, bringing attention to creativity will help you figure out what works best for you to inspire more creativity.

- When we actively put on our "creative hats" and decide to be creative, sometimes ideas will surface that could not otherwise emerge.

- Creating with others can often inspire new ideas and connections we are not able to make on our own.
- You may be surprised by what you come up with. This will build your confidence to continue creating.
- When you celebrate actions you've taken and ideas you've had as being creative, this can help us form a new narrative of our own capabilities, potentially leading to new opportunities in life.
- Recognizing and acknowledging the creative work of others more often helps us build connections to colleagues, people we admire, and to younger creatives for whom affirmation may be remembered throughout their lives.

 YOUR CREATING MONOTASK

Solo Brainstorming!

For this monotask, we're going to do three short exercises to come up with some fun new ideas. These tasks are *not* about actually making these things happen in the world. For now, they are just about bringing our focus to the creative parts of our brain and tuning out everything else.

Getting ready:

- Set aside thirty minutes in total — that's ten minutes for each of the rapid-fire monotasks below. The idea is speed, not depth.

- Creating can take some time to warm up, so it's best to do all three monotasks below in one sitting.

This approach will ideally help you get some creative momentum going.

- Find a place where you won't be interrupted. Put your phone down, with notifications turned off.

- Put on some music if it helps you get excited about being creative — if you don't know whether music helps you, try silence first, then experiment with different types of music in the background.

- Do sixty seconds of physical activity to get your blood flowing before you sit down. Jump up and down a few times, swing your arms, jog in place, or something like that.

- Write your ideas down on a notepad — in ink! Be confident.

Monotask 1: Write down five ideas for a novel, a movie, or TV series. Spend ten minutes on this task.

- There are no limits on where you can take this. You can write down ideas for an action movie, a thriller, a science fiction epic, a romantic comedy, a police procedural series, a nature documentary, or just about anything else. Or maybe you have an idea for a mystery novel, a work of historical fiction, a coming-of-age story, a children's book, or something else that pops into your head. We've all consumed a lot of entertainment in our lives and you probably have had your own ideas for what might make a good creation over the years — this is the time to write them down.

- The plot, setting, or characters can revolve around something you know a lot about, or be something you want to research and explore.

- If you're stumped for ideas, think about your life, family, town, workplace. Even if it's not a complete story, start with a character, conflict, setting, or feeling and write that down as one idea. If making up a fictional idea is too daunting, write down true stories you would want to tell — a person you want to write a biography about, a scientific idea you want to explore, or history you want to dive into.

Monotask 2: Brainstorm five ways you want to change the world. Give yourself another ten minutes for this one.

- Draw a line down the middle of a page. List five problems you would like to address on the left side and five possible solutions on the right side.

- The problems you choose to address might be along the lines of poverty, healthcare, addiction, divisive politics, cancer, or climate change. Or they can be challenges you've encountered personally -- mean people, sleep deprivation, food allergies, and so on. Perhaps you want to find a cure for a disease, create a more affordable version of something, or improve educational systems.

- Your solutions might include educational campaigns, technological innovations, nonprofit organizations to start, research, fundraisers, or anything else.

- The ideas can be big or small. The solutions can include changes you want to make in your life — go vegan, volunteer more often, or recycle more. Or they can be wild and ambitious — a national bedtime, solar panels on every home, or free something for all!

Monotask 3: Generate five ideas for what you would do if you weren't so busy or didn't need to earn a living. Ten more minutes can be spent on this task.

- The ideas could range from different careers you want to pursue, something you want to learn or go back to school for, trips you want to take, artistic endeavors you would love to explore, people you'd like to spend more time with. You can write truly anything down.

- Don't spend any creative time on reasons you *can't* do these things. If you feel any negativity (such as regret that you haven't done these yet), let it go. This exercise is not about *how* you will do these things, it is about *what* you would do if you had zero constraints on your time, resources, or capabilities.

- Focus *all* your thinking on positive, creative thoughts, limitless possibilities, and fun adventures.

- Maybe you want to write a novel that you thought of in Monotask 1. Or spend time with your grandkids, travel to India, volunteer more often, or find a cure for cancer. Don't limit yourself.

Congratulations — you just came up with fifteen creative ideas! You are creative.

If you struggled to come up with ideas, try taking a break and repeating one of the previous ten monotasks in this book. Doing this will bring your attention to a different point of focus, taking the pressure off you to create. Overall, try to relax and *think less*; the goal is for the creative ideas to flow.

The next chapter is about thinking, which is a separate monotask from creating. Let's try to separate the two and not overthink creating.

Ideas can all be shaped and refined later; the first step is to give birth to them.

Your Mantra: "Now It Exists!"

How amazing is it that we can all create something and then proclaim, *Now it exists!*

Look for opportunities to say this mantra as you celebrate your creativity.

The Urge to Multitask

Some of the actions you take to encourage creativity will possibly resemble multitasking. Examples of this might include brainstorming while out on a walk or listening to music while painting. The key is to be clear about which of these is your primary task and which is your background task.

Time pressure can lead to multitasking our creativity with other activities. Since we have so little time available in our lives, we might be tempted to always do two things at once—thinking about a story we want to write while at work, for example. Many combinations will simply lead to being less effective at both tasks—you may end up with a story that is not well thought-out and work that is not your best quality.

Look for opportunities to multitask in a positive way, such as doing something creative alongside your kids while they do their homework—you will still be parenting, and they will see you as a good role model and creative inspiration. Or ask your supervisor if you can take on a creative project at work, such as rearranging the break room or organizing the holiday party. Make the case for why it's valuable to them and why you are capable of executing it.

Your devices are very powerful in their ability to help you create, but they can also become sources of distraction and wasted time. During your creative time, turn off notifications and close apps and windows that are not essential to your creative work. Advertisers and other companies want you to pay attention to *their* creative ideas—instead, cultivate the ability to resist them and redirect your attention to monotasking *your* creative ideas.

Waiting until you have enough money to pursue a creative path full time can be frustrating and also lead to constant multitasking while you work at a job you don't love just to pay the bills. Take some time to think deeply (monotask *thinking*!) about whether you could make a living with your creativity if you truly monotasked it. If you can't live a fully creative life right now, look for ways to be creative on a regular basis—volunteer at an art fair, teach in a field of interest, or build a website to showcase your portfolio. Just make sure to always do one thing at a time with your full focus.

Self-doubt can also be very harmful to our creative aspirations and can lead to multitasking in order to avoid failure with the one thing we really want to do. Instead of working one job or focusing on a single project, we might take on several at a time, often out of economic necessity, but other times out of a fear of failure in one concentrated effort. Instead of pursuing one new idea and putting all of our energy into making it successful, we hedge our bets and spread ourselves thin across multiple concepts that don't pan out or have mediocre results.

Try to resist the temptation to always be doing more. Focus on one thing at a time and do it well.

The Reinforcements

Big Magic: Creative Living Beyond Fear by Elizabeth Gilbert is one of my favorite books about living a creative life. In it, Gilbert dispenses a lot of good advice such as, "Recognizing that people's reactions don't belong to you is the only sane way to create. If people enjoy what you've created, terrific. If people ignore what you've created, too bad. If people misunderstand what you've created, don't sweat it." Her book might inspire you to find ways to integrate more creativity on a regular basis!

Reinforcing creativity is important, and also highly personalized. Sometimes you should take a direct route, and other times you need to take a very indirect approach. Neuroscientists Mark Beeman, PhD, and John Kounios, PhD, authors of *The Eureka Factor: Aha Moments, Creative Insight, and the Brain,* found that creative breakthroughs often require distracting your mind away from a problem you are trying to solve. This is certainly an argument for more play, sleep, taking breaks, and adding variety to your life.

Best-selling author Tess Gerritsen finds that she frequently reaches her "Eureka!" moment in book plotting from behind the wheel of a car on long drives: "Something about the act of driving seems to open up my mind to answers," she says. While on the surface this might sound like multitasking while driving, it is possible that the monotasking focus we bring to driving is what enables other parts of our brains to make creative insights in the background.

Here are some ideas for reinforcing creativity. For additional suggestions, see monotasking.tips.

- Do new activities and see new sights—newness encourages our brains to adapt and make new neural connections; it can be through these connections that we discover original ideas and inspirations.
- Travel—even to a neighboring town—is a great way to be exposed to lots of new things—sights, foods, and people.
- Get outside your comfort zone: Take a painting class, join a writing group, or read a how-to book on just about any subject (e.g., baking, gardening, or playing the banjo).
- Write your ideas down in a creative journal and come back to them every once in a while.
- Move your body, exercise, get outside.
- Experience other people's creations for inspiration— movies, musicals, books, TED Talks. All of these and more can stimulate your creativity.
- Establish a creative space at home, or somewhere else where you can go to create, ideally on a daily or weekly basis.
- Set aside creative time.
- Cultivate positive encouragement—make friends who are good at supporting your creativity. Don't be afraid to share ideas with them, listen to their ideas, and support each other.
- Be gentle on yourself—try ultimately to be fueled by your inner motivation. Savor the feeling you get when you look at your work and say *Now it exists.*
- Don't give up. Creating can be hard work.
- Make yourself accountable—announce to someone what you are going to do and have them check in on your

progress; this can also be referred to as an
"accountability partnership." If you have someone
waiting to read your chapters, or celebrating milestones
you achieve on a new project, you will have more
motivation to be creative and productive.

- Celebrate your creativity—don't worry about every idea
  turning into a moneymaker or a success story. Celebrate
  little creations and the big ones, too. Go out for dinner,
  buy yourself a small gift, frame your creation, find some
  way to mark the occasion.

- Start somewhere—don't worry about how messy or
  complete your ideas are. All ideas have to start
  somewhere; rarely do they arrive in a finished state.

- Allow yourself to be bored! In our modern world, with
  smartphones in hand, we almost never have to be bored
  when we don't want to. However, there can be an upside
  to boredom. In *Bored and Brilliant: How Spacing Out Can
  Unlock Your Most Productive & Creative Self,* Manoush
  Zomorodi writes, "Boredom is the gateway to mind-
  wandering, which helps our brains create those new
  connections that can solve anything from planning
  dinner to a breakthrough in combating global warming."

The Task in Your Past

Think of all the creating you did as a kid, even if you didn't like some
of it. Art projects at school or things you made in the backyard. Papier-
mâché. Popsicle stick sculptures. Chalk on the driveway. Putting
stars on your ceiling. Staging a play.

Maybe you came up with some creative moves on the playground or basketball court. Or made up some creative excuses to
get out of school or something you didn't want to do. Perhaps it was
an ingenious science experiment, an original argument in an essay,

or an inventive twist on a research project. A musical solo. A great joke. A new cupcake flavor or cookie decoration.

We all did a lot of creating earlier in our lives. It happened naturally—we were just being kids and having fun. Connect with your inner creative and try to bring some of that creativity back into your adult life. It might be with a coloring book, a trip to a local pottery or painting studio, or resuming an old hobby that you used to love.

Famous Creators

Vincent van Gogh produced more than nine hundred paintings in his lifetime, but only sold one, possibly two, while he was alive. While his genius is now recognized, he struggled financially and psychologically. He wanted to achieve fame, but he primarily created out of the need to make art and present his unique vision of the world. No matter how ahead of its time it was and how little commercial success he had, van Gogh never abandoned painting.

On the other hand, Charles Dickens wrote fifteen novels, including *David Copperfield*, *Oliver Twist*, and *A Tale of Two Cities*, and was paid extremely well while he was alive. The need for money to pay for his lifestyle (and avoid the poverty of his childhood), was a primary motivator for his creativity.

Grandma Moses (Anna Mary Robertson Moses) became famous for her paintings despite not beginning to paint until she was seventy-eight years old! In 1843, Ada Lovelace wrote the first computer program. Madame Curie devoted her life to life to scientific discoveries; her research into radiation was pioneering and creative.

Creativity doesn't have to make money, be on Broadway, or change the world. The joy of creating things that don't exist is wonderful. We should all do more of it.

FOCUS, STILLNESS, AND CREATIVITY

If you've taken a yoga class, you've probably heard the teacher say something along the lines of "Try to be fully present, right here, right now, on your mat." They usually say that right when my mind has drifted off to some- where else — how did they know? The reality for me is that a lot of creative ideas come to me while I'm practic- ing yoga, maybe because of the calmness of the environ- ment, or maybe the ideas are trapped somewhere in my body and I need to move around to get them to percolate up to the surface.

It's easy to say the words that you should focus, be present, and do one thing at a time, but it's hard to actu- ally do it. The mind wanders at yoga, just like it does everywhere else, perhaps even more so in a peaceful set- ting where your mind quiets and lots of thoughts then rush in to fill the silence. The multitasking that happens in these situations is generally all in your head as you think about something that's bothering you, work you have to do, or have a flash of creative inspiration.

Of course, I can't make notes at yoga when I get a cre- ative idea — it would be inappropriate to bust out my phone or a stack of Post-it Notes. I have to have some trust that if a good idea appears, it will come back to me later.

My friend Lauren, a yoga instructor in Boulder, Colo- rado, advises that bringing your attention to your breath is the primary tool to bring yourself back to the present moment and build your focus. The simple but easily overlooked act of noticing a single breath can be a game changer. It can shift your mind from busyness to stillness instantly. In the long run, the focus and stillness you cultivate will help you be more creative.

Yoga, Tai Chi, Qigong, and other practices that combine mind and body can help you slow down, work on your monotasking skills, and potentially boost your creative potential.

How You'll Know You're Good at It

One of my favorite writers, Kurt Vonnegut, was exceptionally creative and encouraged creativity in others. In his book *A Man Without a Country*, he advised, "Practicing an art, no matter how well or badly, is a way to make your soul grow, for heaven's sake. Sing in the shower. Dance to the radio. Tell stories. Write a poem to a friend, even a lousy poem. Do it as well as you possibly can. You will get an enormous reward. You will have created something."

As Vonnegut advises, just do it—don't worry about what others think. You'll know you're good at monotasking creating when:

- You feel good about the effort you made.
- You make time and space for it in your life on a regular basis.
- You encourage creativity in others. Try to be one of those friends who gives positive feedback.
- You learn more about yourself and what makes you creative—whether it is a direct approach with dedicated

creative time or relaxing your mind so that ideas can pop into your head (or a combination of the two at different times).

What if...

... *you just don't have it?* Lots of people feel this way. Try to remember that every human has the power to create and that creating *anything* that didn't exist before is creating.

... *you can only come up with one idea?* All creativity starts with one idea. It doesn't matter if it's a great idea or just an idea, you have to start somewhere.

... *you get overwhelmed by too many ideas?* Sometimes I get frustrated that I have a lot of ideas but not enough time to pursue them all. To manage this feeling, I've added some structure to my creativity. I try to make note of all my ideas (see sidebar on page 195)—in this way, I'm giving them respect and not letting them evaporate without having a chance. I come back to work on some of them, others I combine into a bigger concept, and a good number I realize weren't worth pursuing after all but I'm still glad I wrote them down.

... *you don't have time or enough hours in the day?* There are lots of opportunities to be creative, you might just have to get creative about it. Make a creative breakfast for your kids, sing on your way to work. Monotask your creativity in small bites, a few seconds or minutes here and there.

... *you think "Why bother, everything that needs to be invented already has been"?* I believe everyone has a unique contribution to share. Even if you don't roll out your creations in a public way, monotask them for yourself and take pride in them.

... *you're planning to create later—on vacation, in retirement, or when you're done with your other work?* I believe in living a balanced life all the time. When it comes to creativity, it isn't something we should *only* do when we have time or money. We can and should be creative as much as possible. This is what will help us achieve our goals and greater happiness in the long run.

Go Create!

I want to read your poems! See the bookshelf you built! Hear about your science experiment!

Give creating your full focus; that's really what matters.

TASK 12: THINKING

We have arrived at the final monotask and you may be wondering, "Wait, was I not supposed to *think* before now?"

You've been doing it right, don't worry. Some amount of thinking goes into just about everything we do.

Thinking is one of the harder monotasks to practice, and that is one of the reasons I saved it for last. Thinking happens in our brains, and we also use our brains for most other activities. It is legitimately hard to separate thinking from everything else we do in life.

Sometimes we think too much when we should just be doing other monotasks. Other times we don't think enough before we act. When we are thinking, it's possible we're not thinking clearly, which can happen for a lot of reasons. Is all of this too much to think about?

Let's simplify what we're trying to accomplish in this chapter so that we can finish strong.

For this final monotask, we really have three objectives:

First, we want to recognize when others are thinking for us and we are *not* thinking for ourselves. In modern life, we have outsourced a significant amount of our thinking to our devices, to algorithms, pundits, influencers, advertisers, news sources, and others. Once we are aware of the thinking that is being done on our behalf, we can decide if it's in our best interests. Then we can selectively reclaim some of the thinking and do it for ourselves.

Second, we want to become more aware of when our attention is being redirected, taking away our thinking time. The more skills we can develop to identify and then resist distractions and multitasking temptations, the better we will be able to think for ourselves when we need and want to.

Third, we want to enhance our ability to separate our thoughts from one another; sometimes our minds are a jumbled mess! To use a Buddhist term, our "monkey minds" are always going in a bunch of different directions at the same time. This has been true for at least as long as humans have observed their own minds, but the accelerating pace of modern life has increased the noise and the clutter. It can be very difficult to manage everything that is in our heads and process our thoughts *one at a time*. The result of all the overload in our brains might lead to procrastination, indecision, anxiety, and other feelings.

We've got a lot of work and thinking to do, so let's get to it.

The Facts About Thinking

There are currently 3.5 billion smartphone users in the world. Pretty much every one of those phones does something for its owner that they used to do for themselves. Before all the apps, algorithms, and websites we have today, we used our brains to do things like remembering and recalling (phone numbers, calendar events, and other facts). We also figured out how to get places without GPS and we made more of our own decisions about what to buy instead of clicking on ads and making impulse purchases. While there certainly are benefits to having technology take care of many of our needs, we should be aware of what we might be losing. What types of thinking are we no longer doing on our own? Are there unintended consequences to letting computers (and the corporations behind them) do so much of our thinking?

Beyond our smartphones, what we see on the news these days

has generally been repackaged to attract maximum attention from us. Where we might have sought out primary sources in the past, or at least processed what we were seeing to come to our own conclusions, much of what we are exposed to now requires very little thought. We frequently skip straight to an emotional reaction, quite often outrage upon seeing the outrage on our screens.

With social media, most of what we see is an algorithm-driven echo chamber that confirms what we already believe. Social media companies use computer programs to present us with more of what we already know and like—this can limit our exposure to new ideas that *inspire* thinking or *require* us to think about what we see. These programs are driven by extensive data that these companies have collected about us—a combination of what we have clicked on, what we have liked, what our friends have clicked on, what else is on our devices, and data from numerous other sources.

‖‖

PANDEMIC-INSPIRED THINKING

When the pandemic was heading our way in March of 2020, I got my notebook out and started writing down all the scenarios that might happen in the coming weeks, and how my business could ride them out.

If the offices of Juniper Books had to close, could we find another way to make and ship our book sets? I listed a few ideas of drop shipping partnerships we could create and how we could reengineer our design and printing processes. If the rest of the company worked from home, could I as the owner go in to pack and ship all the orders by myself? I wrote down questions that needed to be answered. If the economy experienced a prolonged recession, would customers even be interested in our expensive book sets, and what could we do to introduce lower-priced options? I sent some quick brainstorming ideas to my team.

All around the country and the world, many businesses were doing or about to do the same exercise. While businesses in areas prone to natural disasters typically have contingency plans for surviving a hurricane or flood, the pandemic and mandated closures were a new type of crisis that was happening everywhere all at once. Virtually no one had a game plan at the ready.

The pandemic created an urgent challenge for everyone to think through changes and act on them quickly. Some were paralyzed by how quickly the pandemic arrived, how it demanded attention in so many areas at once — keeping our families safe, our children engaged, our businesses operating. Others seized the opportunity to change their business models and some of those companies thrived.

Restaurants pivoted to takeout operations and, later, outdoor seating. Healthcare providers reengineered their layouts and policies to minimize the spread of COVID. Companies came up with all sorts of creative ideas for new products and services, how to sell gift cards, and how to operate remotely. The pandemic required a *huge* amount of thinking on so many levels.

Even when I may be overwhelmed by what is going on in my life and in the world, I've always found it helpful to keep thinking. The ideas I come up with may not be that great, they may be the result of stress or desperation, but at least I feel like I'm doing something and that the world is not completely out of my control.

Why Monotasking Thinking Will Help You Do Everything Better

When we use our brains, we can accomplish just about anything. From the invention of the wheel to space travel, when humans put our minds to a task, we are capable of remarkable achievements.

We can also think our way through a broad spectrum of routine tasks in our daily lives. Thinking about the new marketing plan, what to buy at the store, which friends and family to invite to our next get-together. These tasks don't happen on their own; they happen with thinking. If we can monotask our thinking, we can potentially improve our execution of every task, big and small.

Monotasking thinking can provide benefits including:

Learning about yourself and how you do your best thinking. There is no one correct or best way to think. It requires experimentation and self-observation to learn how you should approach certain types of thinking. Monotasking thinking will help you better understand yourself and how you can be effective.

The ability to operate on instinct later. You could also call this training, practice, or studying. The more we can pay attention while taking a class, learning a new piece of equipment, or practicing a drill, the more we can operate on instinct later. The more we invest in thinking up front, the more we can move forward with less thinking later. Anyone who has experienced an emergency, such as witnessing an injury to a loved one, can relate to what it feels like when you jump into action and know what to do.

Better decision making. Monotasking thinking does not mean overthinking. Indecisiveness and stress frequently accompany overthinking and we want to avoid that. Monotasking thinking is about being aware of when you are thinking, giving it your full focus, and also being aware of when you are overthinking. If anything, monotasking thinking should help you make decisions faster and feel good about them.

Identifying when not to think. Sometimes we do our best thinking while doing something completely different, for example, sleeping or exercising. Monotasking thinking is not only about the mono-tasking itself, but intuitively feeling when you should stop thinking and go do something else—such as playing in order to be more productive and less stressed.

 YOUR THINKING MONOTASK

Go Big, Go Deep

In *Deep Work: Rules for Focused Success in a Distracted World*, author Cal Newport explains, "To produce at your peak level you need to work for extended periods with full concentration on a single task free from distraction. Put another way, the type of work that optimizes your performance is deep work."

Monotasking thinking is similar to what Newport describes as "deep work," an ability that is uncommon in today's world yet highly valuable from a personal, economic, and, I would add, social perspective.

We're going to practice two monotasks. The first one involves thinking about a big idea and observing your thought process. In the second one you will recall a memory, then make a drawing of it — no talent required, only thinking.

Monotask 1: Think about a big idea

To get ready:

- Set aside twenty minutes total. Choose a time when you will be alone.

- Find a quiet space to think. If you are inside, close the windows and minimize outside noise. Turn off all music and sound.

- Put your phone on Do Not Disturb (you may want to have it nearby later in the exercise).

- Get a notepad and a pen.

Now, you're ready to do some deep thinking about an idea that most people don't know that much about or think about often. *This should feel out of your comfort zone, and that's okay.*

- Think about this idea for about five minutes:

  - The universe is constantly expanding.
  - The farther you travel from Earth, the faster things move away from us.
  - This has been going on for billions of years.
  - The distances between galaxies, black holes, stars, planets, and whatever else is out there is immense.
  - The speed at which objects move in different directions is incredible — some at hundreds of thousands of miles per hour.
  - How is it possible that we're able to sit here, read a book, and make notes while the universe is expanding so violently and rapidly in every direction?

- Spend ten minutes writing down your thoughts. These can be about anything related to the idea above — perhaps your thoughts have something to do with gravity, time, the beginning of the universe, the end of the world, astrophysics, philosophy, religion, the meaning of life, space exploration, extraterrestrial life — truly whatever comes to mind.

- This exercise is not about knowing anything about science; it's about dedicating time to thinking and observing your thoughts.

- You can make a list, create a drawing, write a short story, or record your thoughts in any medium that works for you. Feel free to use your phone to capture a voice memo or make a video while you think through your ideas.

- Try to observe your thought processes as you proceed through different types of thinking — digesting the big idea, contemplating your response, generating quick ideas that come to mind, developing deeper concepts with more focused thinking, articulating your response.

- Is it hard to concentrate? Are other unrelated ideas popping into your head?

- After you have documented your thoughts, take about five minutes to look through your notes and see if you can learn something about your mind and how you think.

- You can repeat this exercise as many times as you like with other ideas. Observe how your thinking process evolves as you pay more attention to it.

Visit monotasking.tips for more big ideas to think about.

Monotask 2: Recall a memory
To get ready:

- Set aside twenty minutes.

- Find a quiet space to think that also has a flat surface to draw on. Choose a time when you will be alone; you don't want someone interrupting you by looking over your shoulder or asking what you are doing.

- Bring a few sheets of paper and a pencil or a pen. A sketch pad or paper in a journal will also work well.

- Put your phone in another room, turn off or close all nearby devices.

- For this exercise feel free to play music in the background.

Now you're ready to think and draw your thoughts from memory.

- Think about a happy place in your past — it could be a home or apartment, a place you visited, a school you went to, or anywhere else that brings back happy memories.

- Now make a drawing of it. Spend twenty minutes on your drawing.

- The idea is *not* to test your drawing talent; it is to access your memories, then figure out how to translate them into a visual representation that exists *outside* of your brain.

- Can you see the space clearly in your mind? Are you unsure of how to represent it on paper? Jump right in and get started anywhere; often the process will flow once you start drawing.

- Do you know what memory you want to illustrate, but can't recall enough detail to complete the drawing? Try closing your eyes and *visualizing* the memory instead of *thinking* about the memory.

- Do not bring up photos you have of the space; the idea is to access the memories in your head. Think of this monotask as one way we can reclaim some of what we have outsourced to our devices. The *real memory* of our experiences is in our brains and that is what we want to work from.

- Draw a floor plan or aerial view of the space if your mind works that way, or that is how you remember it—understanding the spatial relationship of one part to another can be important in our memories.

- Make a note of colors if you recall them or if they are important. Grab some markers or simply label the colors you remember.

- If people or animals are important, draw those, too.

- Use multiple sheets of paper or start over a few times if you get into a groove and need a fresh start on a clean page.

- When you are finished, take a few minutes to reflect on your drawing.

- Were you able to draw all of the thoughts that came to mind, even if only in a rudimentary way? What part of this was hard or easy? Did the process of drawing stimulate more memories to flow as you worked on the drawing?

Your Mantra: "Think, [your name here], Think!"

We can all use a reminder to think sometimes. Our mantra for this monotask is designed to put us into thinking mode, and to encourage us to think harder when we are there.

Think, Thatcher, think! That's what I tell myself when I need to push myself to think, or to think harder. I repeat this mantra while writing, when managing my business, and often when navigating a variety of social and familial situations.

You can use this mantra to remind yourself to think when deep work is required and you need to come up with your best ideas and solutions. Use it to create some distance between your devices and the thinking they usually do for you. Use the mantra to tune out all the influencers, pundits, and know-it-alls and instead come up with your own conclusions.

The Urge to Multitask

One of the reasons it is especially tempting to multitask while thinking is because no one can see you thinking. You do it in your brain, and so it's your own little secret that you are thinking while doing something else.

We think about going to the gym while we are at work. We think about work while exercising at the gym. We think about the errands we need to run while socializing with friends. We think about socializing with friends while running errands. There are many times where our body may be in one place, but our mind is elsewhere. These are internally driven multitasking distractions. Some are harmless, but when we choose to monotask, we can do everything better.

Many distractions are generated somewhere on our devices while we use them for other tasks. It may be a notification that pops up, an email that comes in, or some clickbait on a website. The cost of these disruptions is not only the time it takes to look at or work on the distraction (text, email, etc.) but also the time it takes to cognitively return to the original task and resume what we were doing — some studies estimate this at more than twenty minutes per diversion. Personally, I think that's a low estimate; online tangents can easily occupy hours of our time.

Advertisers and the media have enhanced the art of clickbait in recent years. One moment you're working on a presentation or a report, the next thing you know, you read "You won't believe what they look like now!" and suddenly you're looking at photos of childhood celebrities who had plastic surgery. Clickbait is *not* designed to fully satisfy you or give you everything you want — the goal is to give you just enough that you'll want more, then the cycle of interruptions continues.

Whether you get lured by clickbait or you decide to answer a text instead of doing the work you need to do, be aware that the deck is stacked against you. Companies are spending billions of dollars and have thousands of workers coming up with ways to attract our attention constantly and repeatedly with easy, pleasurable diversions. Your best defense is to reclaim control of your attention through monotasking.

The Reinforcements

Paying attention to something makes it more interesting to us, and that can be a reinforcement to our thinking monotask. In *Finding Flow: The Psychology of Engagement with Everyday Life*, Mihaly Csikszentmihalyi explains, "If you are interested in something, you will focus on it, and if you focus attention on anything, it is likely that you will become interested in it. Many of the things we find interesting are not so by nature, but because we took the trouble of paying attention to them."

In addition to being able to control and direct our attention to what is interesting and important in our lives, it's good to have a big bag of tricks to help reinforce focused thinking. What works for someone else may not work for you. What once worked for you may lose its effectiveness or might not be right for the thinking you need to do at a particular moment.

Here are some strategies that may help reinforce your thinking time, whether it be studying, working, general problem-solving, or creative work. Heads up—this is a long list; don't overthink which reinforcements to use or try to do everything at once!

- *Background sound.* Some people think best in silence, others need some music or noise in the background; find what works for you. For different types of thinking, you may want different music, sounds, and to experiment with volume levels.
- *Headphones.* Some people find that headphones, especially over-the-ear headphones, even if they are not playing music, have a focusing effect. They can also signal to other people that you are concentrating and don't want to be interrupted.
- *Setting.* Where you do your thinking has a big impact on how much you get done and the quality of your thinking.

Just because your friend gets their best work done at a loud coffee shop buzzing with activity doesn't mean it will work for you.

- *Caffeine.* Speaking of coffee shops, some people do their best thinking with the help of caffeine. Don't overdo it—if you consume too much caffeine, you'll get jittery and may not be able to focus or sit still. Take breaks for a few days every now and then.

- *Ergonomics.* Make sure you are comfortable and that your physical positioning does not distract your brain from the work it needs to do. Set your screen to the proper height, experiment with different chairs, or use a standing desk.

- *Time of day.* Observe what time of day you do your best thinking and arrange your schedule accordingly. Keep a journal to track when you do your best thinking. Is it related to the time of day or when you wake up (including from a nap), or is it affected by meals?

- *A step-by-step plan.* Don't try to do everything at once. If you're tackling a big problem or large assignment, break it apart into components that you work on and complete before moving on to the next part.

- *Cooling off.* Sometimes jolting yourself with cold water in the sink or shower, or cold air from outside, can help shake things up and stimulate thinking!

- *Sleep.* Make sure you get enough rest; our brains need it to do our best thinking!

- *Experimentation.* No matter what, keep experimenting throughout your life to see what works best to inspire your best thinking. Try sketching ideas, recording yourself talking about them, or journaling your thoughts.

- *Reading and monotasking.* One way to prime your brain to do some focused thinking is to do some reading first, or to practice one of the other monotasks. This will help bring your attention to where you need it to be.

- *Settling in.* Whenever and wherever you are doing your thinking, take a moment to arrive and settle in. Close your eyes, take a deep breath, let go of everything else besides what you need to think about right now.

- *A change.* If you are having a hard time thinking, take a break, go for a walk, get some fresh air, play a musical instrument for a few minutes, or make some art. All of these can help stimulate a shift in our brains that may allow us to come back with a fresh perspective and ability to be productive.

- *Thinking together.* Depending on what you are working on, it can be helpful to brainstorm or talk through your ideas with other people. Observe whether this works for you or if you are a better solo thinker. If you are working with others, just make sure that someone is responsible for writing down the good ideas that you produce.

The Task in Your Past

Thinking is a critical part of our entire life, but our ability to think in different ways evolves as we grow up. How we thought as children differs from how we think as adults.

It's amazing to reflect on how our thought processes have developed since birth. We've learned to not only generate complicated and sophisticated ideas, but also how to give language to them.

Developmental psychologist Jean Piaget did pioneering work on cognitive development and established that *children think differently than adults.* As infants we were limited to sensory perceptions.

During our early years, we learned language, but didn't yet understand more advanced concepts like logic or empathy. By the time we were seven to eleven years old, we understood more complicated arguments around known events, but hypothetical discussions were still outside of our grasp. It is only after we entered our early teen years that we began to develop reasoning and planning.

Understanding how far we have come in our individual lives, how much we have learned, and how much more sophisticated we are now in our thought processes can really help us put our brains to work. We can continue to develop our thinking as we grow older, using our experiences to inform our ideas. But that development won't necessarily happen at the same pace or depth if we regularly outsource much of our thinking to devices and other people.

Those who grew up in the era before the ubiquity of the internet and devices had a fundamentally different experience developing thinking skills than humans born in the twenty-first century are having. The long-term effects of screens and smart devices on the development of the brain and our ability to think is a subject that will be studied for many years to come. Since we don't know what the future holds, for now let's connect to what we do know about ourselves and our past experience of clearer, less distracted thinking.

Deep Thinkers

When Joe Dispenza was twenty-three years old, he was hit by an SUV during the biking stage of a triathlon. Six of his vertebrae were broken and doctors recommended a complex surgery that, if successful, might have left him partially disabled and facing a life of chronic pain. He turned down the surgery and proceeded to heal himself by visualizing a completely healed spine in his head for two hours a day, *thinking* through all the steps required to put it back together.

Nine and a half weeks after the accident, he was completely recovered. He tells this story in *You Are the Placebo: Making Your Mind Matter*, as well as the stories of other individuals who healed themselves through the power of their minds. Dispenza also gives examples of people who *thought* they were sick, and so they *became* sick, even when there was nothing wrong with them. The idea that our thoughts can be so powerful that they heal our bodies, or make us ill, is fascinating.

Before writing the plots for *The Hobbit*, *The Lord of the Rings* trilogy, and *The Silmarillion*, J.R.R. Tolkien first created multiple Elvish languages and hand drew numerous maps detailing the geography and landmarks where his characters lived and traveled. He wanted to understand the distances to be covered, their relationship to each other, and avoid confusing readers or inadvertently creating inconsistencies. The world he created was deeper and more realistic as a result of the thinking that went into the novels before they were even written. Tolkien's attention to detail established a new process that future fantasy writers would follow to make their worlds more believable.

In 2020, the Tour de France was won by a twenty-one-year-old Slovenian named Tadej Pogačar on the penultimate day. He overcame a deficit of fifty-seven seconds during the twenty-two-mile time trial with an incredible demonstration of fitness, determination, and a healthy dose of thinking. In his post-race interview, he explained how he won: "It was not just me, we did the recon, I knew every corner, every pothole, where to accelerate on the road..." While many other elite athletes and their teams have made use of thinking over the years in order to gain an advantage over their competition, Pogačar's victory was historic and unexpected. It was not considered to be a time gap that he could make up against his rivals after three weeks of all-out racing around France. Research, preparation, and thinking may have made all the difference.

THINKING AND ACTING UNDER PRESSURE

The summer after I graduated from college, I went on a backpacking trip in Alaska for twenty-eight days with NOLS (National Outdoor Leadership School). There were about sixteen students plus three instructors, and we didn't see any other people for pretty much the duration of the expedition. We hiked about eight miles a day, through forests, over alpine tundra, and across numerous streams and rivers. We carried and cooked our meals, slept in tents, and tried not to think about how bad we smelled after so long without a shower!

About two-thirds of the way and a hundred miles into the trip, our lead instructor broke her leg while crossing a river. She had been our fearless, inspirational, and extremely knowledgeable guide for about eighteen days, but now she was in extreme pain, and clearly needed to get to a hospital as soon as possible.

Everyone on the trip quickly grasped that we had to switch immediately from adventuring and playing to thinking and action in service of getting her evacuated safely. The other two instructors put together a plan — we would set up camp for the night, and keep the injured instructor as comfortable as possible while we pursued two approaches to get help.

One small group of the fastest hikers would prepare to hike out and get help the next day — it was about a dozen miles to the nearest road. The second plan was more of a long shot — one of the uninjured instructors would broadcast an emergency message throughout the night using a line-of-sight radio. The hope was that an airliner high over Alaska would pick up our distress call—this was before satellite phones were routinely taken on such expeditions.

What happened over the eighteen hours following the accident was an amazing combination of thinking and operating on instinct. Few of us had trained for an emergency such as this. Two previously goofy teenage boys turned out to be extremely handy at building a stretcher out of backpacks. The rest of the group assumed other responsibilities — setting up tents, cooking for everyone, and reviewing topographical maps to plan the hike out.

The sound of a propeller plane landing on a gravel bar at sunrise the next morning was one of the most beautiful noises any of us had ever heard. All of the thinking that NOLS and the instructors had done before the trip, combined with the thinking we did on the fly after the accident happened, had paid off. A Japanese airliner passing overhead had heard our message and relayed the transmission to the NOLS base in Alaska. They in turn dispatched a plane to bring the instructor to the hospital. Ten days later, when the rest of us got back to base camp, we learned that she had been through surgery on her broken leg and was on her way to recovery — what a relief!

How You'll Know You're Good at It

Faster thinking often comes from focused thinking. You can accelerate your processing (like a faster computer) when you dedicate yourself to monotasking thinking—you will be able to take in more information and make sense of it faster. You will be making new connections in the synapses in your brain when you think and learn. We are all capable of becoming better thinkers throughout our lifetime: Our ability to get better at thinking does not end at any specific age.

Sometimes we make bad decisions when we are in a rush or not paying attention. If we can monotask thinking and really pay attention, we can think things through and arrive at better decisions most of the time. Well-thought-out decisions tend to be healthier, more considerate of others, and generally better for everyone in the long run. You'll know you are good at monotasking thinking when:

- You can stay focused on your thinking tasks even when there are distractions swirling around you. The ultimate goal of monotasking is to be able to decide on your own where to apply your attention, not be whipsawed around by others and multitasking temptations.

- You can really arrive, settle, and stay focused on thinking through what you need to do. The seventeenth-century French philosopher Blaise Pascal once said, "All of humanity's problems stem from man's inability to sit quietly in a room alone." It can be a real challenge to sit still and do anything these days when there is so much to do all the time.

- You don't shy away from thinking about big questions and complicated things. In *Stillness Is the Key*, author Ryan Holiday explains, "We have to get better at thinking, deliberately and intentionally, about the big questions. On the complicated things. On understanding what's really going on with a person, or a situation, or with life itself."

- You can reclaim some of your abilities to find information periodically without Google or other sites. You will also be able to make more of your own decisions and remember more details and important information.

What if...

...you overthink things? Some of us tend to overthink things. It's no surprise that overthinking can lower your productivity, block your creativity, and shake your confidence. Simple tips to help reduce overthinking include limiting the amount of information you're taking in and setting a deadline for decisions. For some, talking over ideas with another person can help; for others, that adds to the indecision. Try to put things in perspective — ask yourself how much does this really matter? If you're moving or changing jobs, yes, you need to take time to consider many things. But try not to overthink what to have for lunch or what socks to wear.

...you have a headache and it hurts to think? If headaches are occasional and you can put off thinking, do it — relax, have some hot herbal tea, and do whatever you can to make your head feel better. If you have chronic pain, of course consult professionals for advice and treatment, which may include having your eyes checked. When I had chronic headaches for years, I did my best thinking lying down.

Go Think!

Think about anything you like but don't think *too* hard. It's time to celebrate the fact that you have reached the end of the twelve individual monotasking chapters — congratulations!

PART III

PUTTING IT ALL TOGETHER

MONOTASKING OUR LIVES

ow that we've talked about each of the twelve monotasks on their own, let's take a brief tour of what it looks like to monotask life on a daily basis, replete with all the distractions, interruptions, and multitasking temptations that exist in the world.

I have described a number of scenarios below that you might recognize. Whether or not you see yourself in these examples, the point is to envision that monotasking is possible in every part of our lives. There will always be distractions and multitasking temptations, but we can make a choice to monotask.

Work

Our goals at work may include being productive, accomplishing our assignments, and making progress in our careers. We probably want to reduce stress, both for ourselves and others. We hopefully also want to be valued team members, good managers, and inspiring leaders.

Monotasking can help us achieve these goals. Dedicated thinking time can be rewarding, both for the ideas we generate as well as the work we complete when really focused. Monotasking listening, to our customers and coworkers, may help us identify opportunities as well as build relationships. Monotasking creativity can lead to better problem-solving, as well as better products, strategies, and plans.

Keep in mind that you will constantly be interrupted, as you always have been! Just because you have decided to monotask does not mean that the phone calls, emails, and notifications or demands from coworkers, customers, managers, family, and friends will stop.

On the other hand, just because the phone rings or an email arrives doesn't mean *you have to drop everything to answer it.*

Monotask your work—bring your full attention to one thing at a time, then move on to the next task. Your work will benefit from your attention and monotasking efforts.

Home and Family

Home and family are extremely important but can often be a source of stress and anxiety. There is typically a never-ending list of things to do, and some family members can trigger our worst behaviors and feelings.

Monotasking can help us try to change things. We can use monotasking to get our work around the house done faster. We may find that monotasking listening leads to positive changes in our previously difficult relationships. Getting more sleep ourselves, and encouraging others to do the same, will also yield benefits at home.

Just because you are monotasking doesn't mean that everyone else will magically start doing the same, or that they will stop interrupting you. It can be hard to find the time to do everything at home that life asks of us. It can be particularly difficult to give your children your full attention when you're working at home as well. Try teaching your children to monotask in small doses; be a role model for what it looks and feels like *not* to be distracted by your devices all the time. Make an effort to combine your playtime with theirs—go for a bike ride, make some pottery, or sing silly songs.

It will not be easy—new habits take time to form, and you will need to be patient and persistent for change to occur.

Relationships and Friends

Utilizing almost all of the monotasks at various times, monotasking can help us make new friends and develop stronger relationships. If you are single and looking for a partner, my best piece of advice is to work on your listening skills! Listening makes people feel valued and will allow you to learn new things about the person you're with.

Now, it's not always rainbows and unicorns—your presence, focus, and monotasking won't necessarily be reciprocated. The other person may not be a good listener, or they might be easily distracted. Sherry Turkle explains the downside of one persistent form of multitasking in *Reclaiming Conversation: The Power of Talk in a Digital Age.* "Every time you check your phone in company, what you gain is a hit of stimulation, a neurochemical shot, and what you lose is what a friend, teacher, parent, lover, or co-worker just said, meant, felt."

Everything is a practice opportunity for monotasking. Monotask your get-togethers. Don't bring your phone, or keep it out of sight and reach. Make an agreement to work on being present together; perhaps even repeat one of the monotasking exercises with a friend.

If it's a persistent issue that a friend or partner is not paying as much attention to you as you are to them, then consider whether it's a healthy relationship for you. Remember that *who* you give your attention to is up to you—it's not unlimited, so direct it wisely.

Hobbies and Sports

It's fun to have hobbies, to exercise and get in shape, to play music, and to make and fix things. Life is interesting—there is so much to do that generally we don't have enough time to do it all.

Monotasking can help us give our hobbies and physical activities more focused attention so that we enjoy them more and maybe get better at them, too. Whether we are playing, learning, teaching, creating, or traveling, we can monotask in order to maximize our happiness and fun.

Distractions and multitasking temptations will continue to come your way even after you've committed to monotasking your interests. You may be in a yoga class and simultaneously thinking about work, playing tennis and remembering something you forgot to buy at the store, or making jewelry in your garage when interrupted by a family member with a question.

Try to stay focused on what you are doing, acknowledge the distractions, and gently steer yourself back to your monotask. Hobbies and sports get us out of our heads and away from our work and daily routines. They can really help refresh and recharge us so that we can be more effective in other parts of life.

Causes You Care About

Monotasking can help make the world a better place. Monotasking a cause does not mean that you have to work on it and only it your entire life. What it does mean is that when you do bring your attention to it, you are focused, you do that one thing (whether it is giving money, writing letters, making calls, protesting, etc.), and you do it well.

By bringing our attention to causes we care about, we can *see* where the world needs our contributions of time, talent, and support. We may also identify where our actions are *not* in alignment with our values. This may lead to monotasking changes in our own lives, such as recycling more, making donations to organizations we have researched, volunteering at a food bank, or working on a political campaign.

The above examples are just a few of the ways that we may seek to positively influence and change the "outer environment" of the world we live in. In *Stand Out of Our Light: Freedom and Resistance in the Attention Economy*, author James Williams writes, "Future generations will judge us not only for our stewardship of the outer environment, but of the inner environment as well. Our current crisis does not only come in the form of rising global temperatures, but also in our injured capacities of attention. Our mission, then, is not only to reengineer the world of matter, but also to reengineer our world so that we can give attention to what matters."

While you make progress by monotasking all of the causes you care about, the world may not go along with you. Some people may be opposed to what you are doing and some may not even understand it. The attentional demands of work and home, and technological interruptions will also get in your way.

Don't be discouraged—every positive change starts with one person. If you bring your attention to something, others will eventually follow, and a larger shift can occur.

Monotask Everything!

Everything can be monotasked.

When you're wondering if you can monotask something, simply remember these two steps:

1. **Take everything away until there is one thing left.**

2. **Bring your focus to that one thing and do it well.**

THE MONO FUTURE

We may think we are busy now, but we're likely to be even busier in the future. Given the trajectory of modern life, we will likely need to work harder to maintain our lifestyles in the years to come, we will interact with bigger and more powerful corporations, we will need to adapt to more technology, and we are certain to experience more sophisticated distractions.

Reflecting on the challenges people face today in controlling their time and attention, Adam Alter quotes design ethicist Tristan Harris in *Irresistible: The Rise of Addictive Technology and the Business of Keeping Us Hooked*: "The problem isn't that people lack will-power; it's that 'there are a thousand people on the other side of the screen whose job it is to break down the self-regulation you have.'"

Acknowledging how hard it is to juggle everything right now and the fact that there might be ten thousand people on the other side of the screen in a few years, how will we keep up in the future?

What if...

... we could focus and apply ourselves to achieve real effectiveness in our lives and in the world? Could we solve climate change, address systemic racism, send a manned mission to Mars?

241

Could we get that promotion? Finish getting a degree? Or, more immediately, can we get our children off their devices and to the dinner table on time?

I truly believe that the process of solving all problems starts with deciding to pay attention. What gets in the way of attention are distractions. All of the distractions in the world, big and small, inhibit our ability to pay attention—as a consequence, our effectiveness at solving problems is diminished.

Many of the newest distractions that have proliferated, especially on social media, are intended to sow division and misinformation. Zeynep Tufekci writes in *Twitter and Tear Gas: The Power and Fragility of Networked Protest*, "Whereas a social movement has to persuade people to act, a government or a powerful group defending the status quo only has to create enough confusion to paralyze people into inaction."

Confusion is certainly a powerful form of distraction. The idea that distractions alone are enough to change the world by causing *inaction* is important to recognize. It happens every day around the world, in ways big and small. We're constantly bombarded with distractions to the point where we cannot and do not get things done.

If we can return ourselves to the present moment, focus on one thing at a time and tune out the technology, distractions, and confusion, we have more potential than we may realize.

We need to redouble our efforts to identify distractions and resist them.

We have to retake control of our own attention.

We need to do one thing at a time so that we can do everything better.

To Multi or Mono

The temptation to multitask doesn't ever go away. We have to be able to recognize multitasking temptations when we see them and have strong monotasking muscles at the ready when we need them.

I hope this book has helped you build strong monotasking muscles and that you can put them to work when you need them.

Thank you for giving me some of your attention—I know how valuable it is.

ACKNOWLEDGMENTS

Writing and publishing a book that an author hopes will change the world takes a lot of hard work, a good amount of luck, and a lot of support along the way. While I have done my best to monotask my part of the process, the magic really happens when others pay attention and get involved.

A couple years ago, *The Twelve Monotasks* was just an idea. Then a synchronicitous conversation I had with Amy Foster set me on the path to making it a reality.

My literary agents at Dupree Miller took it from there, believing in me and the potential of this book. Nena Madonia Oshman enthusiastically shepherded *The Twelve Monotasks* to its ideal home at Little, Brown Spark. Ali Kominsky worked tirelessly to help me make the book the best it could be and position the book to have a positive impact on the world. Thank you to Jan Miller for all of your guidance and sage advice.

The team at Little, Brown Spark have been a writer's dream to work with. My editor, Marisa Vigilante, provided the perfect balance of positive reinforcement and suggestions to make the book stronger. Jessica Chun, Stephanie Reddaway and everyone on the Little, Brown marketing team applied their talents to bringing the message of monotasking to a wide audience.

Thank you to Heather Neyer and Natalie Coleman, members of my Juniper Books team, for creating the final cover design. Michael Noon and everyone on the Production team at Little, Brown graciously evolved the look and feel of the book to optimize the reader's experience. Thank you to Kathryn Carroll at Hachette Audio and Dan Bittner for your work on the audio book.

Numerous readers provided feedback on various drafts of *The Twelve Monotasks* and their feedback made it stronger. Thank you to Laura Burleson, Annie Melton, Hal Clifford, Ben Leroy, CJ Bartlett, Elizabeth Lane, Ellie May Harris, Carol Fries, Jim Enright, Joan Hall, Scott Bocim, Deb Cerio, Patricia Paige Cronin, and Lily Iserson. A very special thank you to Sara Henry for getting involved at a pivotal time and encouraging some of the biggest improvements to the manuscript.

While I conducted research, the conversations I had with Virginia Santy, Lauren Lewis, Ed Han, Paola Balsa, Mark Goulston, Nicholas Carr, Casey Schwartz, Philip McKernan, Emily Basurco, Amanda Marks, and Joey Coleman were particularly helpful and influenced my thinking in various ways. Thank you all for your time and insights.

Writing the book required me to be away from the office for extended stretches. A special thank you is due to Sandra Greenway, Kirsten Herzig, and Heather Neyer for managing Juniper Books and minimizing distractions for me during this time period. Thank you to my entire team at Juniper Books for your hard work, creativity, and attention to detail in recent years, especially through the pandemic with all of its challenges.

As I share in the book, there have been a lot of ups and downs in recent years. I want to thank Kirsten Carpenter, Barry Wine, Winnie Abramson, and Susan Wine for all of their support and our many conversations, during this time. To Bob Ransom, thank you for your work on monotasking.tips and for all of your marketing suggestions. To Amelia Winfrey, thank you for listening, for all of your feedback, and for reminding me to monotask!

And last but not least, my children, Cedar and Jasmine, influence and inspire me every day. Thank you for being you, thank you for being there for me, and thank you for appreciating the attention I give you and knowing that I am here for you.

CHAPTER NOTES

THE ART AND SCIENCE OF MONOTASKING

Monotask: Dictionary.com, n.d.

The word "multitasking": "IBM Operating System/360 Concepts and Facilities," IBM Systems Reference Library, File Number: S360-36. bitsavers.org/pdf /ibm/360/os/R01-08/C28-6535-0_OS360_Concepts_and_Facilities_1965.pdf.

Apple's Macintosh computer: Tony Long, "Jan. 24, 1984: Birth of the Cool (Computer, That Is)," *Wired*, January 24, 2008. wired.com/2008/01 /dayintech-0124/.

A 2011 study: Michael N. Tombu, Christopher L. Asplund, Paul E. Dux, Douglass Godwin, Justin W. Martin, and René Marois, "A Unified Attentional Bottleneck in the Human Brain," *Proceedings of the National Academy of Sciences* vol. 108, 33 (2011): 13426–31. doi:10.1073/pnas.1103583108 .pnas.org/content/108/33/13426.

Keeping up with social media: Melissa G. Hunt, Rachel Marx, Courtney Lipson, and Jordyn Young, "No More FOMO: Limiting Social Media Decreases Loneliness and Depression," *Journal of Social and Clinical Psychology* vol. 37, no. 10 (2018): 751–768.

"If you're not paying": Larissa Rhodes (Producer), Jeff Orlowski (Director), *The Social Dilemma,*. United States: Exposure Labs, 2020. Spoken by Tristan Harris.

TASK 1: READING

"And with this invention": Maryanne Wolf, *Proust and the Squid: The Story and Science of the Reading Brain*, Harper Perennial, 2008.

The Pew Research Center: Andrew Perrin, "Who Doesn't Read Books in America?," Fact Tank, the Pew Research Center, September 26, 2019. pewresearch.org/fact-tank/2019/09/26/who-doesnt-read-books-in-america/.

Further, younger people tend to read: Bureau of Labor Statistics, U.S. Department of Labor, "Average Hours Per Day Spent in Leisure and Sports Activities…2019 Annual Averages," *The Economics Daily*, 2020. bls.gov /opub/ted/2020/men-spent-5-point-5-hours-per-day-in-leisure-activities -women-4-point-9-hours-in-2019.htm.

"Reading has been shown": Ceridwen Dovey, "Can Reading Make You Happier?," *The New Yorker*, June 9, 2015.

"The mere presence of these devices": Adrian F. Ward, Kristen Duke, Ayelet Gneezy, and Maarten W. Bos, "Brain Drain: The Mere Presence of One's Own Smartphone Reduces Available Cognitive Capacity," *Journal of the Association for Consumer Research* vol. 2, no. 2, April 2017. journals .uchicago.edu/doi/full/10.1086/691462.

"Reading is still the main way": Katherine Rossman, "Bill Gates on Books and Blogging," *The New York Times*, 2016. nytimes.com/2016/01/04 /fashion/bill-gates-gates-notes-books.html.

"Why has the physical book endured": Nicholas Carr, Juniper Books Annual Catalog, 2017.

"If you only read": Haruki Murakami, *Norwegian Wood*, Vintage, 2010.

TASK 2: WALKING

"I went to the woods": Henry David Thoreau, *Walden*, Everyman's Library, 1992 (1854).

"I think that I cannot": Henry David Thoreau, *Walking*, Tilbury House Publishers, 2017 (1862).

The Centers for Disease Control and Prevention, "More People Walk to Better Health," 2012. cdc.gov/vitalsigns/walking/index.html.

Mintel found a big jump: "Sports Participation: Inc Impact of COVID-19 — UK," 2020.

According to the Arthritis Foundation: Arthritis Foundation, "12 Benefits of Walking." arthritis.org/health-wellness/healthy-living/physical-activity /walking/12-benefits-of-walking.

Philip McKernan: Interview with author, 2020.

"Walking animates and enlivens my spirits": Jean-Jacques Rousseau, *Confessions Book IV*, 1731. knarf.english.upenn.edu/Rousseau/conf04.html.

TASK 3: LISTENING

"In the act of listening": Ralph G. Nichols and Leonard A. Stevens, "Listening to People," *Harvard Business Review*, 1957. hbr.org/1957/09/listening -to-people.

"It struck me that this": Casey Schwartz, *Attention: A Love Story*, Pantheon, 2020.

Adam Bryant, author of *Quick and Nimble*: Adam Bryant. "How to Be a Better Listener," *The New York Times* Smarter Living, n.d.. nytimes.com /guides/smarterliving/be-a-better-listener.

"Babies who are": Diane Rich, "Listening as a Way of Life," the National Children's Bureau leaflet. Retrieved from lx.iriss.org.uk/sites/default /files/resources/Listening%20to%20Babies.pdf.

In many Native American communities: Joan Tavares Avant, "Talking Stick and Feather: Indigenous Tools Hold Sacred Power of Free Speech," *Indian Country Today*, August 15, 2017. indiancountrytoday.com/archive /talking-stick-and-feather-indigenous-tools-hold-sacred-power-of-free -speech-HIxdWMdV60CeaMvIVwfqnA.

"The Talking Circle is": John Peters (Slow Turtle), 1979, as quoted in Avant, "Talking Stick and Feather."

"Seek first to understand": Stephen R. Covey, *The 7 Habits of Highly Effective People*, Free Press, 1989.

"Deep listening": Jillian Pransky, "Practice Deep Listening to Change Your Stress Response & Start Truly Receiving Yourself," *Yoga Journal*, September 12, 2017. yogajournal.com/yoga-101/restorative-yoga-101-practice -deep-listening-to-changeyour-stress-response.

AWOL: Mark Goulston, interview with author, 2020.

TASK 4: SLEEPING

The former CEO of Yahoo!: Max Chafkin, "Yahoo's Marissa Mayer on Selling a Company While Trying to Turn It Around," *Bloomberg Businessweek,* August 4, 2016. bloomberg.com/features/2016-marissa-mayer -interview-issue/.

Margaret Thatcher served: Tom de Castella, "Thatcher: Can People Get By on Four Hours' Sleep?" *BBC News Magazine*, April 10, 2013. bbc.com/news /magazine-22084671.

"Sleep is the single most effective thing": Matthew Walker, *Why We Sleep: Unlocking the Power of Sleep and Dreams*, Penguin Random House, 2017.

The CDC: Centers for Disease Control and Prevention, "Short Sleep Duration Among American Adults." cdc.gov/sleep/data_statistics.html.

"Routinely sleeping": Ibid.

Being tired also leads: Brian Tefft, "The Prevalence and Impact of Drowsy Driving," *AAA Foundation for Traffic Safety*, November 2010. aaafoundation.org/prevalence-impact-drowsy-driving/.

The National Safety Council estimates: The National Safety Council. nsc.org/.

"Never leave that till tomorrow": Benjamin Franklin, *Poor Richard's Almanack*, Peter Pauper Press, 1980 (reprint).

"Rest doesn't just magically appear": Alex Soojung-Kim Pang, *Rest: Why You Get More Done When You Work Less*, Basic Books, 2016.

In Washington Irving's: Washington Irving, *Rip Van Winkle and Other Stories*, Dover Publications, 2018 (1819).

In Ottessa Moshfegh's: Ottessa Moshfegh, *My Year of Rest and Relaxation*, Penguin Press, 2018.

"These two threads": Ariana Huffington, *The Sleep Revolution,* Harmony, 2016.

"Generally it is recommended that sleep medications": Troy Farah, "What Science Says About Using Sleep Medications," *Discover*, August 20, 2019. discovermagazine.com/health/what-science-says-about-using-sleep-medications.

TASK 5: EATING

According to the Bureau of Labor Statistics: Bureau of Labor Statistics. bls.gov/news.release/atus.t02.htm.

Meal replacement companies like Soylent: Arwa Mahdawi, "I Tried Soylent, Silicon Valley's Favourite Foodstuff. It's Everything That's Wrong with Modern Life," *The Guardian*, September 11, 2018. theguardian.com/commentisfree/2018/sep/11/i-tried-soylent-silicon-valleys-favourite-foodstuff-its-everything-thats-wrong-with-modern-life.

Now, tasty energy bars: "North America Energy Bar Market 2018-2023—Rising Demand for Clean-label Products," PR Newswire, May 24, 2018. prnewswire.com/news-releases/north-america-energy-bar-market-2018-2023—rising-demand-for-clean-label-products-300654271.html.

The local food and slow food movements: "USDA Farmers Market 2019 Rules and Procedures and Operating Guidelines," 2019. ams.usda.gov/sites/default/files/media/USDAFarmersMarketRulesandProceduresandOperatingGuidelines.pdf.

Research on establishing new habits: Phillippa Lally, Cornelia H. M. van Jaarsveld, Henry W. W. Potts, and Jane Wardle, "How Are Habits Formed: Modelling Habit Formation in the Real World," *European Journal of Social Psychology* vol. 40, no. 10 (October 2010): 998–1009. onlinelibrary.wiley.com/doi/abs/10.1002/ejsp.674.

"Do we really want": Anthony Bourdain, *Kitchen Confidential*, Bloomsbury Publishing, 2000.

"Gastronomy is the reasoned": Jean Anthelme Brillat-Savarin, *The Physiology of Taste*, the Folio Society, 2008 (1825). Translated by Anne Drayton. This edition follows the text of the 1994 reprint by Penguin Books.

TASK 6: GETTING THERE

Historically, people have been willing: Jonathan English, "The Commuting Principle That Shaped Urban History," *Bloomberg*, August 29, 2019. bloomberg.com/news/features/2019-08-29/the-commuting-principle-that-shaped-urban-history.

"A 2017 study found": "Long Commutes Costing Firms a Week's Worth of Staff Productivity." Mercer, May 17, 2017. uk.mercer.com/newsroom/britains-healthiest-workplace-flexible-working-and-commuting.html.

"The Zebra found": Taylor Covington, "Distracted Driving Statistics, Research, and Facts," *The Zebra*, August 18, 2020. thezebra.com/research/distracted-driving-statistics/.

"The consequences of distracted driving": National Highway Traffic Safety Administration. nhtsa.gov/risky-driving/distracted-driving.

All drivers were replaced by computers: Yuval Noah Harari, *21 Lessons for the 21st Century*, Random House, 2018.

"Nothing is so simultaneously familiar": Jenny Odell, *How to Do Nothing: Resisting the Attention Economy*, Melville House, 2019.

On his late-night show: Katherine Schaffstall "James Corden Responds to Viral Clip Showing He's Not Driving During 'Carpool Karaoke,'" *The Hollywood Reporter*, January 30, 2020. hollywoodreporter.com/news/james-corden-responds-carpool-karaoke-clip-him-not-driving-1274919.

"I did not tell half of what I saw": Marco Polo, *The Travels of Marco Polo*, Everyman's Library, 2008 (reprint).

"Travel is fatal to prejudice": Mark Twain, *The Innocents Abroad*, Library of America, 1984 (1869).

"Life offers you a thousand chances": Frances Mayes, *Under the Tuscan Sun*, Broadway Books, 1997.

"Two roads diverged in a wood": Robert Frost, *The Road Not Taken: A Selection of Robert Frost's Poems*, H. Holt and Co., 1991.

TASK 7: LEARNING

"If a brain is exercised properly": Michael Merzenich, *Soft-Wired: How the New Science of Brain Plasticity Can Change Your Life*, Parnassus Publishing, 2013.

The Finnish Geriatric: Miia Kivipelto, et al., "The Finnish Geriatric Intervention Study to Prevent Cognitive Impairment and Disability," *Alzheimer's & Dementia*, Vol. 9, No. 6 (2013): 657–665. Retrieved from pubmed.ncbi.nlm.nih.gov/23332672/.

As John Basinger: Lois Parshley, "This Man Memorized a 60,000-Word Poem Using Deep Encoding," *Nautilus*, May 29, 2018. nautil.us/blog/-this-man-memorized-a-60000_word-poem-using-deep-encoding.

"In the beginner's mind": Shunryū Suzuki, *Zen Mind, Beginner's Mind: Informal Talks on Zen Meditation and Practice*, Weatherhill, 1970.

"Whether chemists, physicists": David Epstein, *Range: Why Generalists Triumph in a Specialized World*, Riverhead Books, 2019.

VARK framework: "Introduction to VARK." vark-learn.com/introduction-to-vark/.

"In the end, mastery": Josh Waitzkin, *The Art of Learning: A Journey in the Pursuit of Excellence*, Free Press, 2007.

TASK 8: TEACHING

According to the World Bank: World Bank, "Number of teachers across education levels," 2015. ourworldindata.org/grapher/number-of-teachers-across-education-levels.

More than 85 percent of users: YouTube Internal Data, Global, 2017. thinkwithgoogle.com/data/learning-related-youtube-statistics/.

TASK 9: PLAYING

We work about four hundred hours": OECD, Hours worked (indicator), 2020. doi: 10.1787/47be1c78-en data.oecd.org/emp/hours-worked.htm.

The U.S. Department of Health and Human Services: https://health.gov/sites/default/files/2019-09/Physical_Activity_Guidelines_2nd_edition.pdf.

In Finland, the government recommends: Timothy D. Walker (June 2014). "How Finland Keeps Kids Focused Through Free Play." *The Atlantic.*

"Recess is associated with": Anthony D. Pellegrini and Catherine M. Bohn-Gettler, "The Benefits of Recess in Primary School," *Scholarpedia* Vol. 8, No 2 (2013): 30448. scholarpedia.org/article/The_Benefits_of _Recess_in_Primary_School.

A class at Stanford: dschool.stanford.edu/classes/from-play-to-innovation.

"With analog gaming": David Sax, *The Revenge of Analog: Real Things and Why They Matter*, Public Affairs, 2016.

"I've found that just saying": Ingrid Fetell Lee, *Joyful: The Surprising Power of Ordinary Things to Create Extraordinary Happiness*, Little, Brown Spark, 2018

"A state in which people": Mihaly Csikszentmihalyi, *Flow: The Psychology of Optimal Experience*, Harper & Row, 1990.

David Beckham first got into: Press Association, "Build It Like Beckham," *The Guardian*, February 2, 2014. theguardian.com/football/2014/feb/02 /beckham-lego-calm-football-star-stress.

In their spare time: Pema Bakshi, "21 of the Most Unexpected (And Strange) Celebrity Hobbies," *Elle Australia*, November 2, 2020. elle.com.au/celebrity /celebrities-with-surprising-hobbies-23780.

TASK 10: SEEING

In the 1970s: Sam Carr, "How Many Ads Do We See a Day in 2020?" PPC Protect, April 9, 2020. ppcprotect.com/how-many-ads-do-we-see-a-day/.

Today, digital marketing: Jon Simpson, "Finding Brand Success in the Digital World," 2017. forbes.com/sites/forbesagencycouncil/2017/08/25/finding -brand-success-in-the-digital-world/#22b27d5a626e.

"Our changing technological environment": Matthew B. Crawford, *The World Beyond Your Head: On Becoming an Individual in an Age of Distraction*, Farrar, Straus and Giroux, 2015.

TASK 11: CREATING

"Indeed, knowledge that one will": Howard Gardner, *Creating Minds: An Anatomy of Creativity as Seen Through the Lives of Freud, Einstein, Picasso, Stravinsky, Eliot, Graham, and Gandhi,* Basic Books, 2011.

More than 100: Omnicore, Social Media Benchmark Report, 2020. omnicoreagency.com/social-media-statistics/.

YouTube reports: Christos Goodrow, "You Know What's Cool? A Billion Hours," YouTube Official Blog, February 27, 2017. blog.youtube/news -and-events/you-know-whats-cool-billion-hours.

"Etsy boasts of 4.3 million active sellers": Etsy, Inc. Fourth Quarter 2020 Financial Results, 2020.

There were 1.68 million books self-published in 2018: Kinga Jentetics, "Self-Publishing Market Review," Publishdrive, December 17, 2019. blog.publishdrive.com/self-publishing-market-review-2019/.

3D printing is a $10 billion market: "3D Printing Market by Offering (Printer, Material, Software, Service), Process (Binder Jetting, Direct Energy Deposition, Material Extrusion, Material Jetting, Powder Bed Fusion), Application, Vertical, Technology, and Geography—Global Forecast to 2024," October 23, 2019. marketsandmarkets.com/Market-Reports/3d -printing-market-1276.html.

"Here's to the crazy ones": "Think Different," Apple TV advertisement, 1997. First version narrated by Steve Jobs.

"No matter what your age or your life": Julia Cameron, *The Artist's Way*, TarcherPerigee, 1991.

"Recognizing that people's reactions": Elizabeth Gilbert, *Big Magic: Creative Living Beyond Fear*, Riverhead Books, 2016.

Neuroscientists Mark Beeman: John Kounios and Mark Beeman, *The Eureka Factor: Aha Moments, Creative Insight, and the Brain*, Random House, 2015.

"Something about the act of driving": Tess Gerritsen, "A Must-Read Book for Writers: IMAGINE by Jonah Lehrer," Tessgerritsen.com, July 9, 2012. tessgerritsen.com/a-must-read-book-for-writers-imagine-by-jonah -lehrer.

"Boredom is the gateway to": Manoush Zomorodi, *Bored and Brilliant: How Spacing Out Can Unlock Your Most Productive & Creative Self*, St. Martin's Press, 2017.

Ada Lovelace: Erik Gregersen, "Ada Lovelace: The First Computer Programmer," Brittanica.com, n.d. britannica.com/story/ada-lovelace-the-first-computer-programmer.

"Practicing an art, no matter how": Kurt Vonnegut, *A Man Without a Country,* Seven Stories Press, 2005.

TASK 12: THINKING

There are currently 3.5 billion: "Number of Smartphone Users Worldwide from 2016 to 2023, Statista, n.d. statista.com/statistics/330695/number -of-smartphone-users-worldwide/.

"To produce at your peak level": Cal Newport, *Deep Work: Rules for Focused Success in a Distracted World,* Grand Central Publishing, 2016.

The cost of these disruptions: Gloria Mark, Daniela Gudith, and Ulrich Klocke, "The Cost of Interrupted Work: More Speed and Stress," Proceedings of the SIGCHI Conference on Human Factors in Computing Systems, April 2008. dl.acm.org/doi/proceedings/10.1145/1357054.

"If you are interested in": Mihaly Csikszentmihalyi, *Finding Flow: The Psychology of Engagement with Everyday Life*, Basic Books, 1997.

Developmental psychologist Jean Piaget: The Editors of Encyclopedia Brittanica, "Jean Piaget," n.d. britannica.com/biography/Jean-Piaget.

When Joe Dispenza was: Joe Dispenza, *You Are the Placebo: Making Your Mind Matter*, Hay House, 2014.

"It was not just me": Jonny Long, " 'I Think I'm Dreaming': Tadej Pogačar Reacts to Winning the Tour de France 2020," *Cycling Weekly*, September 19, 2020. cyclingweekly.com/news/racing/tour-de-france/i-think -im-dreaming-tadej-pogacar-reacts-to-winning-the-tour-de-france-2020 -469205,

"All of humanity's problems": Blaise Pascal, *Pascal's Pensées*, E.P. Dutton, 1958.

"We have to get better at thinking": Ryan Holiday, *Stillness Is the Key*, Portfolio, 2019.

MONOTASKING OUR DAILY LIVES

"Every time you check your phone": Sherry Turkle, *Reclaiming Conversation: The Power of Talk in a Digital Age*, Penguin, 2015.

"Future generations will judge": James Williams, *Stand Out of Our Light: Freedom and Resistance in the Attention Economy*, Cambridge University Press, 2018.

THE MONO FUTURE

"The problem isn't that": Adam Alter, *Irresistible: The Rise of Addictive Technology and the Business of Keeping Us Hooked*, Penguin Press, 2017.

"Whereas a social movement": Zeynep Tufekci, *Twitter and Tear Gas: The Power and Fragility of Networked Protest*, Yale University Press, 2018.

INDEX

ABOUT THE AUTHOR

Thatcher Wine is a creative entrepreneur and the coauthor of *For the Love of Books: Designing and Curating a Home Library*. He is the founder and CEO of Juniper Books, a company based in Boulder, Colorado, that specializes in custom curated libraries and beautifully designed book sets.

Thatcher has long been an advocate for reading as a form of self-care and a means to build focus in the digital age, concepts that form part of the foundation of *The Twelve Monotasks*. While defending the place of printed books in our culture for the past twenty years, Thatcher has also sought to reinvent their creative potential. He has spoken widely about books and libraries including a TED Talk called "The Books We Keep, the Stories We Tell."

Thatcher's monotasking philosophy took shape as he grew Juniper Books and weathered numerous personal challenges, including a life-threatening cancer diagnosis. From a childhood in the restaurant business to the rise and fall of his internet startup in his twenties, Thatcher's experiences have informed and refined his ideas on living with focus and purpose.

Thatcher lives in Colorado and loves to spend time with his two children and play on the slopes and trails whenever possible. For more information and to contact the author, please visit monotasking.tips, thatcherwine.com, or juniperbooks.com.